THE DIRTY NASTY TRUTH

18 True Crime Stories and 10 Life in Prison Stories to Stop Juvenile Delinquency

(bullying, youth violence, gangs, shoplifting, insurance fraud, teen drinking and drug abuse)

JOHN BARRETT HAWKINS

DARK PLANET
PUBLISHING

Author — John Barrett Hawkins
Editor — James Bottomley
Typesetting and Interior Design — Cris Wanzer
Cover Design — Armondo Villalobos

© 2013 John Barrett Hawkins

Printed in the United States of America
ISBN 10 # 0979171822
ISBN 13 # 9780979171826
Library of Congress Control Number 2011924359

Dark Planet Publishing books are available at special quantity discounts to use for sales promotions, premiums, or educational purposes. Please contact our Sales Department via our web site:

www.darkplanetpublishing.com

Categories:
Stop bullying, youth gangs, teen drinking, juvenile crime, youth crime, gang violence, youth gangs, stop gang violence, teen gangs, teen shoplifting, teen bullying, youth drinking, youth drug abuse, bullying stories, youth violence stories, prison gangs, prison drug abuse, stop gangs, stop youth violence, stop teen drinking, stop teen drug abuse, stop underage drinking, teen violence, true prison stories, true gang stories, criminal, gang member, youth gang member, race riot, youth authority, murder & mayhem, biographies & memoirs, true accounts, true crime, law, organized crime

Table of Contents

FOREWORD

This book is based on a juvenile diversion outreach program named Convicts Reaching Out to People (CROP) at R.J. Donovan State Prison in San Diego, California. The CROP program was comprised of incarcerated felons who had chosen a positive path for their lives. During the one-day CROP presentations, the felons gave personal testimonies to the youth and the adults who brought them (parents, teachers and juvenile justice personnel). The stories made such an impact on the visitors that lives were changed.

My role in CROP was liaison and sponsor. I am the founder of From The Inside Out Inc. Our main focus is teens at risk of juvenile delinquent behavior. We facilitate intervention programs for first-time youth offenders for the Carlsbad Police Department, teach emotional literacy, and arrange for parents and schools to take kids to the CROP presentations.

My journey to become CROP's community liaison began with a spiritual epiphany. I was working in my garden one afternoon when God spoke to me: "You are going to CROP and you are taking the mayor with you." The message was clear and authoritative. My friend and fellow church member, Dick Lyon, was the mayor of Oceanside, California. I immediately dropped my gardening tools and went inside the house to phone him.

"Hello," Dick answered on the second ring.

"Hi Dick, its Priscilla Steiner."

"What's going on?"

"Do you believe in Divine inspiration?" I asked.

Dick was a deeply spiritual man.

"Yes," he answered without hesitation.

"God just told me that I should monitor a youth intervention program at Donovan State Prison called CROP," I said. "And you are supposed to go with me."

"Well, then it looks like I'm going, too," the mayor replied.

CROP was the brainchild of a prisoner named Jerry Wills.

One year earlier Wills had attended a spiritual retreat called Kairos. Kairos was a four-day Christian fellowship event where a dozen free people, known as "the outside team," went into prison to commune with 30 prisoners. During the course of the retreat, each member of the outside team gave a personal testimony. They stood before the group and spoke about their relationship with God. In between the talks, the outside team members sat at the tables with prisoners where they read bible verses, prayed together, sang songs, and shared stories from their lives. There was no condemnation or judgment; just a weekend filled with God's unconditional love. The Kairos program produced the most amazing transformation of human beings. Wills thought that the Kairos format would be a great way of reaching kids to keep them out of trouble. The twist was that CROP would be based on personal testimonies in which prisoners spoke about their crimes and the lessons learned. Wills crafted a proposal for CROP and presented it to Chuc Cottier, the associate warden.

Cottier and his supervisor John Rattelle, who was the Senior Warden for the California Department of Corrections, were men of character and moral fortitude. They believed in redemption. Both thought that men who had made terrible mistakes could change and become productive citizens again. They encouraged community volunteerism in their prison. In addition to Kairos, they allowed other spiritual groups to work with the prisoners, started AA programs, and even allowed sports teams to come into the prison to compete with the inmates.

Wills assembled a team of 12 prisoners with diverse ethnic backgrounds and criminal histories. The personal testimonies ran the gamut from inner city gang life to white collar crime and drunk driving murder. The program followed the Kairos format of combining personal testimonies with "table time," where the prisoners worked one-on-one with the teens to counsel them away from criminal behavior. In the beginning, CROP worked exclusively with the San Diego police department, who would bring 5-10 youth offenders to the presentations.

Mayor Lyon and I attended a CROP presentation, which ran from 10:00 a.m. until 3:00 p.m. The program's focal point was the personal testimonies. The CROP members spoke to the group with raw honesty about the shameful crimes they had committed.

They spoke with passion, remorse, and regret. Their crime stories were compelling and captivating. Most importantly, the felons were adept at sharing lessons that could only have been learned through painful retrospect. I was completely blown away. Attending that first CROP presentation was one of the most emotionally stirring events I have ever experienced.

Mayor Lyon was awestruck. On the drive home, he said, "Did you see the way those men owned up to their criminal wrongdoings? And how they traced their criminality back to their adolescence? Amazing. This program is one of the most powerful tools for change that I've ever encountered. Why doesn't anyone know about this? We should be taking advantage of this program."

Mayor Lyon's sentiments resonated with my own feelings and became a lightning rod that would change the direction of my life forever. In that moment, I knew that God had inspired me to attend CROP for a reason. In the coming months, that reason became clear. I was destined to become CROP's community liaison.

I was not the kind of person anyone would expect to volunteer in a prison outreach program. I was a lily-white, mother of six who worked as a teaching assistant at the same elementary school my kids attended. I had no experience with gangs or people who broke the law. I didn't even have any friends who did drugs. I had nothing in common with the prisoners. Yet, none of that seemed to matter. What I witnessed at the CROP presentation was life-changing for everyone who attended — adults as well as youths.

The next day at work I approached my son's sixth grade teacher, Sheri. I told her that I wanted to take the entire class — 25 students — into the prison for a CROP presentation. To my surprise, Sheri agreed.

Next, I met with Chuc Cottier, the associate warden. At this point, CROP was not open to the general public. The prison officials had no plans for extending the reach of the program beyond the work they were already doing with the police department.

"Mayor Lyon and I believe this program has immense value for *all* teenagers. My son is in the sixth grade. He's a good kid who doesn't do drugs, hang out with gang members, or commit crimes. But I think he needs this. I think all teenagers need to understand the consequences of poor choices."

Cottier proved to be the right man to oversee the CROP program. He cared about people and recognized the impact the CROP program had in changing the direction of teens that were on a path of deviant behavior. Following a rigorous screening process, Cottier gave the approval for my son's class to attend CROP.

Prior to entering the prison, I held an orientation with the students. I talked to the class about the clothes they would be required to wear, their behavior, and what they could expect. The kids were curious, excited, and apprehensive.

Whatever fear they felt disappeared quickly. From the moment we walked into the visiting room, the felons put us at ease. The prisoners were kind, courteous, and respectful. It was clear that these men knew they were being given a rare opportunity to make a positive contribution. The youths responded to the felons' passion and genuine desire to deter them from making the same mistakes that had cost them their freedom.

I watched the kids as the felons gave their personal testimonies. Every face in the room was spellbound; their mouths were literally gaping as the prisoners told their stories. Sixth-graders are usually restless, with wandering attention spans. But the felons' true crime stories were mesmerizing. *They have their unwavering attention*, I thought. *What a great platform to educate!*

Their teacher concurred.

"That was one of the most unique and enlightening things that I have ever witnessed," Sheri said following the presentation. "You have to do something with this!"

Sheri's response provided confirmation and direction. Suddenly, the light went on. My life was surrounded by children. I worked at a school and had six kids of my own. I remember thinking, *I'm supposed to be working with kids, but this is how I'm supposed to do it.* I was pumped and motivated to take action.

Over the next few months, I arranged for all of the sixth-grade classes at my school to attend CROP. Then I started making phone calls to the principals at middle schools and high schools throughout San Diego County, and arranged for them to attend CROP. Everyone who went to CROP was touched in some way.

The program transcended demographics — age, color, sex, financial stature. The stories the CROP members told were charged with emotion and enriched the lives of every person who was fortunate enough to attend the presentations. Word spread throughout the education community. Teachers lined up to bring their students to CROP.

For four years I worked from home, out of a makeshift office in one of my kids' bedrooms. The costs of running the program and providing transportation for countless teens was funded out of my own pocket. Eventually, a friend named Fred, who was an attorney, helped me file the paperwork to register as a non-profit organization.

I chose to call the organization From The Inside Out for several reasons; the most significant reason being that lasting change for a teen who is involved in anti-social behavior must come from inside. It is here that the CROP program worked its magic. More often than not, something traumatic occurred during the felons' childhoods, such as bullying, peer rejection, or parental abuse, which resulted in them developing low self-esteem. As the felons discussed the root causes of their criminality and the terrible things they endured as children, the teens in attendance became conscious of the pain that was fueling their own raw emotions and poor behavior. From this moment of recognition, real change was possible for these kids.

From The Inside Out evolved from these meager beginnings into an organization that now teaches teenagers emotional literacy. Our main focus is working with first-time youth offenders in conjunction with Carlsbad Police Department's juvenile justice division.

Over the past 20 years I have arranged for thousands of teenagers to attend the CROP presentations. CROP has been directly responsible for the transformation of the lives of countless youths who were destined for a life of crime. It has been a privilege and a blessing to be involved in such an invaluable program. Sadly, CROP was suspended in 2011 because of a reality TV program called "Beyond Scared Straight" that was broadcast on the A&E Network. The TV show revealed unsafe Scared Straight tactics that were being used at other prisons. CROP has never used intimidation to scare kids into shaping up; the program has always followed the story-telling format that Wills modeled from Kairos. Given the liability issues raised by the "Beyond Scared Straight" TV show and the present political climate, I fear the CROP program may be lost forever.

Into the void comes John Barrett Hawkins' book *The Dirty Nasty Truth: 18 True Crime Stories & 10 Life in Prison Stories to Stop Juvenile Delinquency.* John is a former CROP member who I met at a CROP presentation five years ago. He is a gifted speaker and accomplished writer who is driven by a fierce desire to make amends for his past criminal behavior. John's goal in writing this book is to bring the CROP program to the masses.

The Dirty Nasty Truth uses true crime stories to captivate your attention and deliver important lessons for readers of all ages. This book can be a useful tool for parents, teachers, and law enforcement professionals seeking to deter teens from making poor choices. First, the CROP members' stories empower teens to identify painful events that may be fueling their own poor behavior and out-of-control emotions. Recognizing the root causes of negative thoughts and emotions is paramount to any meaningful change. Second, the stories provide a non-threatening, non-judgmental platform for adults and kids to talk about important issues, including drugs, shoplifting, bullying, gangs, sex, and self-esteem.

Enjoy the stories. Learn and grow from your reading experience.

Priscilla Steiner
Founder and Director
ftiosd.org
fromtheinsideoutinc@gmail.com
760-754-0580

CHAPTER 1
Million-Dollar Murder Conspiracy

For as long as I can remember, entrepreneurship has been my passion, my intuitive call to purpose. It has also been my affliction and my fountainhead of pain and remorse.

In 1985, at the age of 22, I partnered with my girlfriend, Alexis Anders, to open a retail clothing store in Lexington, Kentucky named Just Sweats. The business idea had evolved over a three-year period as I observed a California company called Pure Sweat grow from one location to 30 stores. Pure Sweat was founded on a simple concept: it offered the largest selection of basic sweat clothing at the lowest possible prices. To their already winning formula, I added sweatshirts that were screen-printed with more than 100 different university insignias, and provided an artist who would hand-paint custom sweatshirts in acrylic while the customers watched.

The store design for Just Sweats was basic and understated. The carpet was charcoal. There were floor-to-ceiling white shelves on the three interior walls upon which neatly folded sweats were stacked in every imaginable color, illuminated by bright florescent lights. There was one small dressing room, a couple of sales tables on the floor, and a checkout counter. The sweat clothing itself was the décor. The entire storefront was glass and, from outside looking in, Just Sweats resembled a roll of Lifesavers candy.

The Just Sweats grand opening was on Memorial Day weekend. Alexis was a successful model and actress on the soap opera "Another World". Her star power led to much "hometown-girl-makes-good" media coverage. There was a great article about us and the store on the front page of the *Lexington Herald Examiner's* business section, with a photo of me stocking the shelves. Alexis gave interviews with other local news media and the store was packed with customers all weekend. The media gushed over Just Sweats, but more importantly, the customers loved the store. The merchandise was high quality and moderately priced. The in-store artist created unique, personalized designs, and the staff was friendly. It was a warm, festive atmosphere, and the product was soon flying off the shelves. It was clear from the first day that Just Sweats was going to be a phenomenal success.

Neither Alexis nor I had any retail experience, so we sent my friend Stan Lungren, who was an executive at Robinson's department stores in Los Angeles, a plane ticket and invited him to the opening. Stan possessed a wealth of retail knowledge that he was happy to impart to us. He helped us establish the basic operating procedures for Just Sweats and taught the staff effective sales techniques. Stan was quite impressed with the customers' responses to the Just Sweats store and made an unforgettable comment: "I can't believe *you* created this!" I interpreted this as the classic, left-handed compliment, as if he was saying, "Who would have thought a dumb-ass like you could develop such a successful business concept?"

Over the next few months, Stan stayed in touch, calling frequently to see how the business was doing. He wanted to get financially involved and offered to invest the money necessary to build a second location. Due to my inexperience in the retail sales business, our attorney viewed a partnership with Stan as a unique opportunity that I should not pass up. I embraced the attorney's advice, and the partnership was formed. To capitalize on Stan's strengths, I convinced him to quit his job in Los Angeles and to work full-time at Just Sweats running the second store.

Initially, we assumed that college students would be an ideal customer base. The closest large university to Lexington was Ohio State University in Columbus, Ohio. We opened the second Just Sweats store on the Ohio State campus. Like the first store, it was successful from the outset.

It did not take long for any of us to realize that we had created something very special. I was beginning to believe that the Just Sweats success formula could be replicated in cities across the country. As the company's sales increased, so did my dreams. I envisioned Just Sweats becoming a nationwide chain—a giant of the clothing industry.

During a buying trip to Manhattan, I put out feelers for expansion capital. Mark Gallo, the credit manager for Martex, the world's second largest sweat clothing manufacturer, weighed in with a creative two-tier proposal. First, Gallo would pay $50,000 for a 10 percent ownership interest in Just Sweats. Second, Just Sweats would retain Gallo as a credit consultant and pay him $10,000 annually. In this capacity, Gallo would raise Just Sweats' credit line at the mill from $25,000 to $250,000 and extend our credit terms from 30 days to 90 days. Additionally, once we purchased and paid for $250,000 worth of inventory, Gallo would report our good standing to the credit-reporting agency Dunn and Bradstreet. We anticipated that this would cause a domino effect: each of the other three large sweat clothing manufacturers would match the $250,000 credit limit, culminating in a million dollars in supplier credit that we would use to expand the business.

It was an exhilarating time for my partners and me. However, when we met with our attorneys to sign the Gallo deal, an unexpected problem arose. The lawyers took us through several potential scenarios, at one point asking what would happen to Gallo's consulting fee in the event of his death. My response, naturally, was that since he would no longer be performing a service for Just Sweats, the company would simply stop paying the fee. Mark Gallo didn't see it that way. He had raised the $50,000 by taking a second mortgage on his home, and said that he intended to use the yearly $10,000 consultant's fee to pay the mortgage. If he died, his wife would be responsible for repayment of the loan, so Mark wanted her to inherit the annual consultant's fee. When Mark and I both stood our ground, the attorneys came up with a solution: Just Sweats would purchase "key man" life insurance policies on each of the three partners equal to the value of their perspective shares. In the event of a partner's death, his heir would receive the insurance proceeds, and his shares would be returned to the company. All parties agreed to this solution, and we formed a new Ohio corporation with Stan and I each owning 45 percent and Mark owning 10 percent. At this time, Alexis sold her shares back to Just Sweats, earning a 50 percent return on her investment. Little did I know that the agreement based on the key-man life insurance policies would someday destroy the lives of many people. I had unwittingly planted the seed of my own destruction.

Fuelled by the investment from Gallo and the increase in our credit limit, Just Sweats embarked on a massive expansion. Over a three-year period, the company grew to 22 shops and $10 million in annual revenues. This was truly a magical time in my life. I realized that I had been blessed with an extraordinary array of good fortune…and it went straight to my head.

As Just Sweats grew so did my level of confidence in my abilities as a businessman, and that increased confidence inspired a limitless vision of expansion of the company. There was no apparent border between my corporate dreams and me. There was nothing to restrain me; no restrictions, no regulations, no personal commitments or other obstacles to slow me down. There was no barrier between me and my intense desire to build a national brand…except a business partner who suddenly lost his passion for the business, and an incomprehensible loss of moral fiber on my behalf.

In the fall of 1987, the principals of Midway Shoes, a Columbus-based company who owned 700 retail shoe stores, approached us with a venture capital deal. They would pay $400,000 for 10 percent of Just Sweats, and we discussed the possibility that their sophisticated management infrastructure could fuel the rollout of a national expansion.

It was at this time that Stan told me that he wanted to sell his ownership in Just Sweats. He explained that, while he enjoyed building our company, he hated living in Ohio. Stan was gay, and had lived an openly gay life in West Hollywood, California, for more than a decade. Living in Columbus had returned him to the closet. Outside of our corporate office he had no social life. Based on the Midway Shoe proposal, his shares in the business were valued at $1.8 million dollars.

We approached the Midway Shoes people about purchasing Stan's shares in Just Sweats. At first they were interested in becoming full partners in the company. Yet negotiations came to a standstill when the Midway Shoes people announced that they would require two years of audited financial statements before they would make a seven-figure commitment. We had never hired an outside accounting firm to audit our books. And since Just Sweats' fiscal year end was April 30th, it became clear that it would take two years to produce the two audits. Stan didn't want to wait that long.

Over the Thanksgiving holiday, Stan flew to Los Angeles, where he met with one of his old-time acquaintances, Dr. Richard Boggs. Together they hatched a plan to fake Stan's death in order to exploit Stan's key-man life insurance policy, which was valued at $1.45 million. The scheme called for Dr. Boggs to purchase a cadaver from a medical school or hospital morgue, identify the body as his longtime patient, Stan Lungren, sign a death certificate for natural causes, and send the body to a mortuary. They wanted me to become Stan's beneficiary, have the body cremated, spread the ashes at sea, and then file the insurance claims. Stan was ultimately to receive all of the insurance proceeds, from which he would pay the doctor $50,000 for his "medical services." The Just Sweats buy-sell agreement specified that, in the event of a partner's death, the shares would be returned to the previous owner. Therefore, I would gain control of Stan's 45 percent ownership in Just Sweats.

I planned to meet my family in Hawaii at Christmas, so I arranged a one-day layover in Los Angeles where I met with Dr. Boggs. He explained to me that obtaining the cadaver would not be difficult for him, and that if a patient died in his office of natural causes, he was responsible for the death certificate. It all seemed so easy. I had no knowledge of medical schools, hospital morgues, or after-death procedures. Dr. Boggs was a 55-years-old medical doctor with impressive plaques from Harvard adorning the walls of his office, so I believed him. The meeting lasted only five minutes. When it was over, I agreed to participate, and in doing so, changed the course of my life forever.

At the time that I was running Just Sweats, I believed that insurance companies were corrupt, soulless entities, and I felt no moral restraints about fleecing them. My negative perception of insurance companies was based on the callous, underhanded way they conducted business. Insurance company lobbyists are notorious for "greasing" politicians and manipulating lawmakers;

their life insurance salesmen are considered to be conniving in their use of sales techniques designed to entice people to purchase insurance they do not need and may not be able to afford; their claims specialists routinely use loopholes in the contract language to deny coverage for potentially life-saving procedures. Their frequent disregard for the welfare of their policy holders has been established through many horror stories reported by reputable journalists. Michael Moore's movie "Sicko" offered a compelling inditement of the evils that insurance companies have been responsible for. Simply put, I didn't think that anyone would care if I ripped off an insurance company. I foresaw a victimless, white-collar crime.

The fraudulent insurance scheme to buy out Stan was a fiasco from the onset. Over the Christmas holidays I joined my family in Hawaii as we had planned. During my absence, Stan removed $1.8 million from the Just Sweats corporate bank account. The Midway Shoes proposal had recently valued the Just Sweats Corporation at $4 million and the $1.8 million Stan took reflected the value of his 45 percent ownership. The plan was that he would disappear with the money. The $1.45 million in life insurance and an additional $500,000 in theft insurance proceeds would repay the company. Yet Dr. Boggs failed to produce the promised cadaver. When I returned to my home in Columbus, Ohio, after the vacation, our bankers were literally at my doorstep insisting that I explain such a large cash withdrawal. Their demands caught me completely off guard. I was stunned to silence. The bankers naturally assumed that Stan had embezzled the money. I had no explanation and simply played dumb. Our corporate lawyers wanted to call the FBI, but I told them that I thought I could find Stan and convince him to return the money without involving the authorities. Before I could act, the bankers surprised me again by demanding that Stan be unilaterally removed as a shareholder, or they would recall the $450,000 SBA loan they had made to Just Sweats. The lawyers smelled blood in the water and suggested I use the leverage derived from Stan's apparent wrongdoing to buy him out at a bargain price. Under all of this pressure, Stan returned the money to the corporation and sold his shares to me for $200,000. I now controlled 90 percent of the company. Stan cried foul, claiming that his shares in Just Sweats were worth 10 times what I had paid him. Stan was my friend, and I had no intention of taking advantage of him. Privately, I agreed with Stan to proceed with my participation in the insurance fraud and to compensate Stan in the full agreed amount at a later date.

Three months passed, and still Dr. Boggs did nothing. Meanwhile, I returned wholeheartedly to the business of running my company. In April, the owner of Rodeo Mills, one of our primary suppliers, called to tell me that he had just purchased $7 million in sweat clothing at one-third the usual cost. I flew to Atlanta to meet with him. During our time together, he took me to a retail store he had opened. He explained that he was looking for innovative ways to sell overstocked inventory. A partnership was discussed, and I returned to Columbus to develop a presentation. I planned to offer him 20 percent of Just Sweats in exchange for one million dollars of the discounted inventory at his cost, essentially selling him a stake in Just Sweats for nothing more than carrying the credit on a million-dollar inventory purchase. This would enable Just Sweats to immediately open 25 new locations and earn $2 million above our regular profits in the next calendar year. I never had the opportunity to present the deal to Rodeo Mills.

Upon my return to corporate headquarters, I telephoned Stan, who was now living in Miami, to share the exciting news about the Rodeo Mills proposal. I told him to forget the fraud, because in another two years I was going to convert Just Sweats to a public company. My financial advisor had explained that a growth company like Just Sweats would trade at 20-times earnings. With the Rodeo Mills deal and so many new stores, I was projecting $3 million in net profits for the coming year, meaning the business could be valued at $60 million on the public market, and the shares I controlled would be worth approximately $42 million. But Stan was no longer interested in the Just Sweats dream or making legitimate business deals. He revealed that he expected Dr. Boggs to deliver any day. All Stan wanted was to complete the fraud and be paid what we agreed under our original deal. At this time I was of the opinion that the doctor had swindled Stan out of a $25,000 down payment and had neither the intention nor capability of ever delivering the promised cadaver. I reminded Stan that Just Sweats' fiscal year-end was April 30, and said if the fraud didn't happen by then, it was never going to happen. The insurance policy was predicated on the buy-sell agreement, and since Stan no longer owned any shares in the business, I could not justify renewing the policy. I didn't realize I had just galvanized a very desperate man.

Just three days later, on April 16, 1988, I received a telephone call directly from Dr. Boggs. In a professional voice, he informed me that his patient, Stan Lungren, had died in his office of heart failure. I remember thinking, *Holy Shit! The doctor finally acquired the cadaver!* I flew to Los Angeles the next day, where I met with Dr. Boggs. He explained that the L.A. County Coroner was performing an autopsy, but that I should not worry because the cause of death was natural. I then played my role as both executor and beneficiary of Stan's "estate." I had the body cremated and the ashes scattered at sea. After the coroner certified the death as natural, I filed the insurance claim and was paid $1 million three months later.

I flew to Miami to take Stan some of the insurance proceeds. Since he was supposed to be dead, we had only spoken during some brief calls made from a pay phone. Now that the scheme had run its course, he was eager to tell me what had actually transpired. When we met, Stan produced a California driver's license and exclaimed, "This is it."

I didn't comprehend immediately. The photo looked so much like Stan that I thought I was looking at his picture on a fake ID. He then explained that Dr. Boggs had lied to us about knowing someone at a medical facility where he could acquire a cadaver. Once Stan realized this, he compelled the doctor to produce a body by killing an unsuspecting man who resembled Stan. As the harsh reality of what he was admitting began to sink in, I raised my hands up to stop him from speaking further.

In response to the horrified expression on my face, Stan attempted to justify his actions. "You should have seen *it.* Cruising the bars and..."

He used the word "it" to refer to this human being they had killed. I immediately became violently sick to my stomach and ran to the bathroom to vomit. The word "it" rang in my ears as I threw up.

That was more than 20 years ago, and the ringing has never ceased. Stan, my friend, was responsible for murdering a completely innocent man; yet he did not acknowledge the man was a human being. I was terrified, shocked, and disoriented. My body trembled as fear enveloped every fiber of my being. *Run* was my only thought, so I broke away from Stan as fast as I could.

Stan Lungren had always been one of the kindest, most gentle individuals I had ever known. I considered him to be one of my closest friends. The thought of him killing another human being never entered my mind. Dr. Boggs appeared to be an esteemed physician; he drove a Roll Royce and lived in a penthouse apartment. It was inconceivable to me that a doctor would intentionally kill someone. I had always believed that doctors *saved* lives, and wouldn't *take* them.

The truth is that I never once seriously considered the possible, sinister consequences of our fraud scheme. Neither Stan nor Dr. Boggs ever said anything to me about a need to have the body look like Stan. I thought the corpse would go directly from the doctor's office to a mortuary, where it would be cremated immediately, so appearance would be a moot point.

I made the terrible mistake of trusting Stan and Dr. Boggs to carry out the plan in accordance with our original agreement. Many years would pass before I understood why two seemingly normal men would commit a murder. For different reasons, both men were in a state of desperation. Following my arrest, I was allowed to review all of the evidence the police had compiled and I learned that Dr. Boggs was strung out on drugs. He was manufacturing methamphetamines in his office and injecting himself daily. The image he projected of a wealthy, successful doctor, was a façade. He was actually in debt and on the verge of losing everything. Stan's desperation was created when he lost his shares in Just Sweats as a result of the perceived embezzlement that occurred when Dr. Boggs did not produce the cadaver according to the timeframe of the original plan. When I told Stan I could not renew the life insurance policy and would not be able to pay him for the sale of his shares for at least two years, he must have perceived that he would lose everything if the insurance fraud did not happen. Even when considering Dr. Boggs' and Stan's states of desperation, I was shocked to learn that they would resort to murder. It was a nightmare of inconceivable proportions, and I was in the center of it.

I returned to my home in Columbus, Ohio. Just two days later an insurance investigator telephoned my corporate attorney and said the police no longer believed the body used in the insurance fraud was Stan. I panicked. The next day I withdrew a large sum of money from my bank account and fled. I did not stop to contemplate how the authorities would view this course of action. I never imagined they would consider that I was involved in the homicide, nor did I realize what my life would be like without the family, friends, or work I cherished. The police later declared that I ran because the crime was planned as a murder conspiracy from the outset, but that is not true. The L.A. County Coroner had conducted an autopsy and pronounced the death to be natural. There was no body to exhume, so I did not even think that Stan or Dr. Boggs would be charged with murder. I bolted because I was afraid of going to prison for the insurance scam and because of the horror I felt about the murder. I did not know what would happen if there was a trial and I was compelled to testify and tell the truth. It was frightening, and my first instinct was to run and hide.

For the next three years I wandered aimlessly from city to city, town to town, country to country. A profound sense of loneliness, alienation, and shame gripped me. I had deceived my corporate attorneys, participated in an illegal scam that endangered the existence of Just Sweats, lied to my business colleagues, and disrupted all of their lives. I hated myself for what I had done, and I was consumed by the cowardly task of running and hiding from those I had wronged.

I was arrested on the Italian Island of Sardinia and charged with insurance fraud and conspiracy to commit murder. In its extradition request, the State of California stated it would seek the death penalty and included jury instructions, which clarified the law in no uncertain terms: *A member of a criminal conspiracy is guilty of every crime committed by his co-conspirators, even if such crime was not intended as part of the agreed upon objective*

and even if he was not present at the commission of such crime.
Since I never intended to hurt anyone—and was not even aware of
the murder until three months after it happened—I had not
considered the possibility that I could be found guilty of that
heinous crime until I was arrested. Reading the extradition request
compelled me to reevaluate my belief in my own innocence, and I
was now petrified of the possible outcome.

In the dark isolation of the Italian prison cell, I reassessed
my role in the crime. If Stan or Dr. Boggs had informed me that
they were going to kill someone to produce the body necessary to
consummate the fraud, I would not have gotten involved.
However, now that the crime had occurred, I had to face a ghastly
truth: Had I refused to participate in the insurance fraud, the
murder would not have happened. Prior to reading the jury
instructions for conspiracy, I was seemingly incapable of
acknowledging the role I played in the death of a man I had never
met. I rationalized that it was something Stan and Dr. Boggs did
without my knowledge or consent. Yet, now I faced the
inescapable truth that I, too, was responsible.

The extradition request identified the victim as Eddy
White. When I read his name, he became a real person to me and a
victim for the first time. Eddy was 46 years of age when he was
murdered. All of his hopes and dreams were lost because of my
involvement in an insurance fraud. The police theory was that
Eddy had been suffocated. I recalled a time as a kid when I had
been trapped under water and thought about the terror and pain
associated with not being able to breathe. Suffocation is a horrific
way to die. I was responsible for Eddy's agony and suffering.

I was also responsible for the grief and misery experienced
by Eddy's family members. He had parents, a twin brother, and a
sister who loved him. I could not begin to imagine their pain and
anguish. I lamented the fact that, because my cohorts and I had
Eddy's body cremated and his ashes spread at sea, we had denied
Eddy the burial of his choice, and had denied his family a funeral
where they could memorialize his life and mourn his tragic death. I
realized that my actions were callous and cruel, and I felt
deepening shame. At night as I tossed and turned in bed, I dwelled
on the suffering I had caused Eddy and his family. I was consumed

with self-loathing and I was certain that nothing I could ever do would atone for my sins or cleanse my conscience.

Italy's largest newspaper, *Il Journale,* published an article about the crime. On the front page was a large photo of me, a single word type below it: *assassino.* Killer. The article pushed me over the edge. I did not want to live in a world that viewed me as a murder. That night I attempted suicide by slicing my wrists with a razor blade. Fortunately, I was not successful but I was damaged in ways I did not understand at that time.

When I was extradited to America, I faced more shame and guilt as I realized how my actions had affected my family. Newspaper and magazine reporters had written vicious articles that implied my criminal conduct was a result of poor parenting on the part of my mother. Since most of the naïve, general public believes everything reported must be factual and true, this vicious lie publicly humiliated my mother. She had her first of two complete nervous breakdowns and her health has never been the same. During the past 20 years she has suffered a never-ending series of physical ailments. My mother's mental anguish affected her parenting of my sister. Her over-protectiveness had a negative impact on my sister's psychological development. My selfish actions caused terrible damage to my loved ones.

I was also responsible for disrupting the lives of my employees and business associates. When the scandal was reported in the *Columbus Dispatch* newspaper, the bank recalled the $450,000 SBA loan. Without that operating capital, Just Sweats was forced into Chapter 11 bankruptcy protection, endangering 300 people's jobs. The letter I had written to a family court judge describing the Just Sweats' warehouse manager's secure employment was no longer creditable, and he lost custody of his three children. The banker who approved the loan to Just Sweats lost his job and his career suffered. My corporate attorney, who assisted me in procuring the million dollars from the insurance company, had his reputation irreversibly damaged. Numerous companies who did business with Just Sweats suffered because invoices were paid late. The domino effect of destruction was endless. Just Sweats was later purchased by three business men and returned to solvency. Yet, in the interim, countless individuals had their lives damaged or disrupted because of my actions. The number of people I harmed was seemingly infinite.

I was tried and convicted of conspiracy to commit murder and given the mandatory sentenced of 25-years to life in prison. I lost everything: my freedom, my friends, my business, and my self-respect. The guilt, pain, shame, depression, loneliness, and alienation I felt on an ongoing basis were indescribable. I possessed a violent self-hatred because I had hurt so many people…and caused Eddy White to be murdered.

One of the most important talks at the CROP presentations is the talk on choices. Whenever I gave this talk I used the story of my crime to demonstrate how one immoral choice could damage so many people's lives. The lesson that I learned the hard way is, we must consider the consequences of our choices, not only for ourselves, but also for how those choices will affect others.

Following the inmates' talks at CROP, the youths in attendance asked us questions. The question I was asked most frequently is, "Why did you commit the crime?" It was literally the million-dollar question. I'm the man who seemingly should have never crossed the line. My life was perfect. I was living my dream.

In an effort to answer this question and understand the root cause of my criminality, I began to read psychology books. In a book by Harvard researcher Dr. Joan Borysenco, I learned that the decisions we make during our youth form imprints on our brains, and as our choices become repetitive the imprints serve as a reference point for every decision we make later in life.

As I looked back on my youth, I discovered a pattern of low morality. In second grade I cheated on a test in school and got away with it. This behavior was repeated throughout my school years and was also prevalent when I played games or sports, where I frequently cheated to win. Also discovered were patterns of shoplifting, stealing, lying to get out of trouble and general dishonesty. I was the kid who did whatever necessary – lie, cheat, steal or take shortcuts – to get the things he wanted. These behaviors were repeated throughout my adolescence. My brain imprint was that of a person with low morality.

When my business partner approached me with the idea of the insurance fraud, I went right back to that reference point to make my decision. I remember thinking, *Hell yes I want to take a shortcut to achieving my goal of expanding Just Sweats nationwide.* My dream was to open 500 Just Sweats stores from coast to coast. The thought of *not* committing the crime never entered my mind. I was a cheater through and through.

I was also an egomaniac. Never once did I consider the consequences of the insurance fraud for how it would affect other people. All I thought about is what was in it for me. What I sought was massive success and adulation. I was the spokesperson for all of the Just Sweats TV commercials, which were on TV all the time. My face was so recognizable that people referred to me as "the Just Sweats guy" wherever I went.

Business colleagues – lawyers, franchisees, bankers – all patted me on the back for my success at such a young age. I got off on the praise and attention of others. I saw myself as this maverick entrepreneur and my ego wanted attention on a national scale.

I faced the harsh realization that I was an immoral, self-centered person. I hated the man I had become. The despair I felt on an ongoing basis was indescribable. I descended into a deep state of depression. Thoughts of suicide returned and dominated my thinking patterns.

For many years I was lost in the wastelands of shame, guilt, and self-hatred. The book *Man's Search for Meaning* by Dr. Viktor Frankl became a guide to transformation by encouraging me to consider the essential question: What is the purpose of my life? Frankl developed a new type of psychotherapy called "Logo (the Greek word for 'meaning') therapy." He wrote, "Logo therapy regards its assignment as that of assisting the patient to find meaning in life. It attempts to help the patient become aware of what he longs for in the depths of his heart."

What I longed for was redemption; to find some way to demonstrate that I was not the type of person who could knowingly be involved in the killing of another human being, and to atone for my wrongful actions. I began to search for a way to be proactive in repaying this debt to society. In time, this became my mission in life.

Frankl suggested that one of the ways that people could discover meaning in life was by "deriving from guilt the opportunity to change oneself for the better." I took this wisdom to heart.

Guided by a sincere desire to overcome my character flaws and become a better person, I embarked on a 15-year study of personal development literature. My self-help journey began with a process of moral and spiritual development. I learned that humans possess universal instincts for virtues such as empathy, honesty, humility, kindness, forgiveness, compassion, and ethical behavior. I created a daily practice designed to instill these values and make them a way of life. I also conducted an in-depth study of self-healing modalities, including mind-body medicine, holistic health care, and personal fitness training. My literary exploration then shifted to human achievement. I wanted to know everything there was to know about how the world's peak performers identified their callings and the techniques they relied upon to fulfill their purpose in life. I read books by psychologists, spiritual masters, personal coaches, Olympic athletes, top entrepreneurs and Eastern mystics. I studied countless books on the subject of achieving personal greatness, and mined them for insights, ideas, advice, wisdom and success secrets. Along the way I took copious notes and compiled all of the most insightful information into a personal excellence program, which served as my new code of conduct.

I developed a passion for information concerning self-improvement and a desire to share the things I was learning with other people. I became a volunteer mentor in Amity, the prison drug rehab program, where I taught a weekly class concerning holistic health practices and human development. I also guided recovering addicts through my personal excellence program, which consisted of four elements: daily personal fitness training sessions, nutritional counseling, behavior modification, and meaning therapy. I was able to help several men overcome their drug addiction and/or problems with obesity. In the process, I made a significant discovery: depression, illegal drugs (coke, meth, and heroine) and processed junk foods all cause imbalances in three key brain neurotransmitters—dopamine, serotonin, and epinephrine; and balance can be restored naturally through high-intensity exercise. Moreover, I found that in food and drug addition, the neurotransmitter imbalances caused uncontrollable cravings, which could be markedly reduced by eliciting the "runner's high" on a daily basis.

These insights motivated me to do something that I never imagined I would be able to do: write a book. I dedicated the next eight years to writing *Penitentiary Fitness: the Amazing Weight Loss Formula* or *A Bodyweight Exercises and Workouts Training Program.*

The self-improvement authors that I admire most share the common belief that *noble intention* is one of the most powerful forces in the universe. Their common message is summarized as follows: *Everyone is born with unique talents and passions, and when those innate gifts are used for the higher purpose of unity (i.e. to serve others), you tap into powerful attractor fields of consciousness that magnetically attract the individuals and events required to fulfill your purpose in life.* The desire to share this extraordinary world view with others led me to write a second book titled *Dare to Be Successful: A Parable to Find Meaning in Life, Build Self-Confidence, Overcome Low Self-Esteem, Set Goals and Land Your Dream Job.*

My quest for redemption crystallized when I became involved in a youth intervention program called "Convicts Reaching Out To People" (CROP). CROP is a public speaking forum where prison inmates speak before large groups of teenagers and the adults who brought them to the presentations (parents, schoolteachers, and police officers). Each felon stands before the group and gives a personal testimony concerning the crime he committed and the lessons learned. The convicts also speak about other pertinent subjects, including poor choices, bullying, gangs, drugs, life in prison, and self-esteem. CROP is an all-day event where the kids sit at tables with the prisoners in a cafeteria setting. Between the talks there is table time, where the convicts work one-on-one with the youths to ascertain why they are getting into trouble and to counsel them away from criminal behavior.

At one of the first presentations I attended, I spent the day with a 17-year-old boy named Ruben who had been to CROP the previous year. I asked him if the program had a positive impact on any of his classmates. Ruben told me that three gang kids dropped out of their gangs and changed their lives as a result of attending

CROP. One of those boys was Ruben. We spent most of the day discussing his plans to attend college and his goal of becoming a doctor.

This was a profound life-changing event in my life. Ruben enabled me to see that CROP provided a genuine opportunity for me to make amends. It was morally self-evident that I should use the story of my crime and all the people I had hurt as a means of deterring others from breaking the law.

At the CROP presentations I frequently interacted with the juvenile justice police officers and schoolteachers. They were evangelistic about the program's ability to inspire change in teens that were making poor choices and getting into trouble with the law.

One day I was speaking with a teaching assistrant named Dorothy Williams who remarked, "I wish I had a book with all of the CROP members' stories for the students who couldn't come today." I took the idea and ran with it, dedicating the next year to writing *The Dirty Nasty Truth.*

I interviewed dozens of criminals to write this book. A surprising pattern emerged. As will be discussed in Chapter 10, I discovered that low self-esteem was the root cause of the prisoner's criminality in nearly every case. Invariably, something happened during their childhood or adolescence – bullying, peer pressure, parental abuse, etc. – that caused the convicts to experience low self-esteem, which in turn, led to anti-social behavior.

From this insight, I gained a deeper understanding about the effectiveness of the CROP program. As the convicts discussed the terrible things they endured as children, the teenagers in attendance became conscious of the pain that was fueling their own raw emotions and poor behavior. From this moment of recognition, real change was possible for these kids. My hope is that is book can also achieve that result.

In the chapters ahead, you will find 17 true crime stories that were written with a focus on understanding the root cause of each man's criminality. Yet, first you'll find a chapter about life in prison, so would be criminals can see how dark their futures really are.

CHAPTER 2
Life in Prison

As described in the Foreword, the CROP program was not like Scared Straight, where the convicts get in the teenagers' faces and use intimidating tactics to scare them into shaping up; however, my "life in prison" talk was frequently referred to as frightening. I just got up in front of the kids and told them all of the terrible things that I encountered during the 20 years I spent behind bars. It is a series of horror stories that are presented as my top ten reasons why you never want to break the law.

#10: The Culture of Violence
In prison, everything is resolved through violence. It is a culture ruled by racism and prison politics. The inmates self-segregate themselves into four groups: white, black, Mexican, and other (which is everyone else). If you are seen talking to someone of another race for too long, you will face problems. Someone from your own race may stab you with a shank, which is a makeshift knife; or you may get rat-packed, beaten by several men. If you are mixed race, you have to choose a side, and even then there is no guarantee that you will be accepted by the racial group you select. The whites are notorious for attacking "White CRIPs," which are white guys or men of mixed race who are in the CRIPs gang. A black man from a Hispanic gang will face similar issues.

Each race has a "shot-caller" who is the so-called leader. The shot-caller gets a 25 percent cut of any drugs brought into the prison by someone of his race. Most shot-callers are drug addicts who are wildly unstable. If you come to prison, this is the person who will determine your fate.

When a new guy arrives on the yard, he must show his paperwork to the shot-caller. The paperwork, which is generated by the prison administration, describes your commitment offense. If you don't produce your paperwork, or have been convicted of a sex crime or a crime against children, you will be "dealt with." This means that someone from your race will stab you. The person chosen by the shot-caller for this mission is almost always a new inmate on the yard, called a "Fish." By going on a mission, a convict earns respect (makes his bones). Not all missions are stickings. Lesser offenses, such as not paying a drug or gambling debt on time, may only result in three or four guys beating you down on the yard. Prior to going on a mission, the convict will receive a package of drugs that he must put up his butt. This is how all drugs are smuggled into and around the prison. Knowing this, the guards constantly strip-search the convicts. During a strip search you must get completely naked, spread your butt cheeks, bend over, and cough while a guard shines a flashlight at your asshole.

Missions frequently do not go according to plan. Not long ago two skinheads beat up an old white guy and stole his "canteen," which is the bag of food stuffs he purchased at the prison store. The skinheads knew this incident would not be tolerated by the other whites, but they didn't care. They were drug addicts and they needed the money to feed their habit. The shot-caller determined that their punishment for this act would be to send them on a mission to beat up a man named Tom, whose drug debts were not being paid. The two skinheads attacked Tom in a blind spot on the yard where the guards could not see them. Tom was prepared for the attack. He had a razor blade that was melted to a tooth brush, and he slashed both of the skinheads on their faces. Both men were left with ugly, permanent scars.

Prison is a violent place. No one is going to show you any sympathy if you end up here. This isn't some two-hour movie. People are humiliated in prison. They also die in prison. They don't tell you that in the rap songs that glamorize gangs, crime, and prison life.

#9: The County Jail

My county of commitment was Los Angeles. The L.A. County Jail is one of the most violent, inhumane places on the planet. It houses more than 10,000 inmates. Petty criminals, such as shoplifters who are awaiting trial, share cells with convicted murderers. The overcrowding is so bad that eight men are stuffed into a cell designed to hold four. This results in four men sleeping on the floor; two of them next to the communal toilet.

On my first day in the county jail I had a cellmate who had been previously convicted of a double-homicide and sentenced to the death penalty. He was down from San Quentin's Death Row to face trial for another murder he had committed while he was in prison. One of his homeboys brought him a three-foot-long steel bar that was the diameter of my thumb. I watched as he sharpened the edge to a fine point by scraping the bar back and forth along the concrete floor, upon which he had sprinkled Ajax scouring powder. It took about two hours for him to fashion a deadly spear. There was no doubt in my mind that he planned to kill again. Needless to say, I didn't sleep that night. To my relief, I was transferred to a different cell the next day.

The worst thing that happened while I was in the county jail awaiting trial was the murder of a Mexican man who was serving a six-month sentence for his second drunk driving conviction. This guy had never previously been incarcerated, and he was unaware of the racial politics that permeate the California prison system. He was hungry, and a black man gave him some food. For this reason about a dozen Mexican gang members beat him to death that evening. It was the most horrible thing I ever saw.

#8: The Daily Grind

Life in prison is like a sadistic version of the movie *Groundhog Day*. It's the same monotonous events day after day.

The repetitive nightmare begins at 6:00 A.M. with a guard's voice blasting from the loudspeaker: "Morning wake up call. Get ready for chow." Ten minutes later the cell doors open and the madness begins. One hundred convicts are released simultaneously. Your senses are assaulted by the horrific sounds, sights, and smells of the other prisoners. You'll see gang members greeting their homies with bizarre handshakes, hugs, and other phony displays of camaraderie; black men calling each other every conceivable variation of the "N" word, as if it was the coolest word ever spoken in the history of language. Invariably, someone with dragon breath will come up to you and singe your nose hairs with some nonsense you do not want to hear first thing in the morning.

After exiting the building, you will be required to stand in line for about ten minutes, no matter what the weather conditions are. Then you will enter the chow hall, where you will be forced to eat food that is not fit for human consumption. Prison food is awful. The chow hall is loud and tense and dangerous. If a fight breaks out the guards use pepper spray and everyone in the room suffers. Approximately two minutes after you sit down to eat, the guards start yelling, "Time's up." If you do not eat fast enough to please the guards, they will hit the table with their nightsticks, glare at you, and dare you to defy them.

Following breakfast the inmates go to their job assignments, which are always terrible. You might be assigned to work in the kitchen or to clean the showers. If you refuse to work, you will lose privileges and possibly add time to your sentence.

Following eight hours of slave labor, the inmates may go to the exercise yard for an hour or so, depending on when they get off work. Then it's back to the building to get in line for a shower. The wait can be several hours. Most anything worth having in prison will be accompanied by a long wait or some other form of torture. For example, once a week the inmates are allowed to exchange their dirty laundry for clean clothes. After waiting in line for an hour, the clothes you get back may not fit, they may smell funny, or may have a disgusting stain. The monthly canteen experience is even more arduous. If you purchase something from an outside vender, such as books, shoes, or a radio, you will be required to go to a place called R&R, where you will be packed into a small holding cell with 30 other inmates for an extended period of time. Medical is the same way. To receive any medical attention, you will be forced to stand in a small, outdoor cage with numerous other prisoners for several hours. The other convicts will be talking nonstop, usually about prison politics or their "poor me" story about why they should not be incarcerated. It's brutal.

#7: *The Guards*

I would say that most of the guards who work at the prisons where I have been housed are normal people. They just want to get their eight hours in, pick up their paychecks, and go home. But like every other realm of society, there are some guards who are sadistic. In prison the guards have absolute power over your life. They tell you what to do and how to do it all day, every day. If you don't like it, if you don't obey, then you are going to have problems. The guards have the power to write you up for a rules violation, which can add to the amount of time you, have to do on your sentence.

The trouble with absolute power is that when it is given to a sadistic person, it corrupts. About five years ago at Donovan Prison there was a guard who was raping inmates by forcing them to give him blow jobs. One of the convicts who were being violated in this manner got smart. He spit the guard's semen into a napkin and smuggled it to his family at a visit. They took the napkin to the San Diego County District Attorney's office, and filed a civil complaint against the prison. The guard was arrested, tried, and convicted of rape.

Another more brutal abuse by prison guards occurred at Corcoran State Prison, in the Security Housing Unit, which is known as "The Hole" or "The SHU." Prison politics are so bad in the SHU that the inmates have a "fight on site" policy. What this means is that whenever you see an inmate of another race you are required to fight him. In order to deal with the violence, the prison administration adopted two new policies. First, they determined that inmates would be segregated by racial designation at all times; and second, the guards were given the authority to shoot any inmate who started a fight without any consequences to the guard. It was a license to kill.

Some sadistic guards at the Corcoran SHU abused these new policies by setting up staged fights between the inmates and betting on the outcomes. The guards would let two inmates from rival races out into a small recreation area and watch them beat each other up. Sometimes they would shoot them. The guards used mini-14 rifles with nine millimeter bullets that tumbled on impact. Three inmates were murdered by the guards, and dozens more were permanently maimed before the federal government became aware of the abuse and put an end to it. The TV Show "60 Minutes" did a special report on the Corcoran SHU, which was known as *gladiator school*. In the show, Ed Bradley interviewed a Mexican convict who had been shot in the back while defending himself in one of the guards' staged fights. The bullet shattered his spine, paralyzing him from the waist down. In fairness to the guards, it should be noted that eight guards faced murder charges related to the Corcoran SHU gladiator wars and all eight were acquitted. The information above was provided by inmates who survived the nightmares, and by "60 Minutes."

#6: Race Riots & Lockdowns

Due to the racial politics that rule the California prison system, race riots are a common occurrence. They even occur on the minimum security yards. You never know when it is going to happen or who will be involved. It could be Blacks against Mexicans, Native Americans against Whites, CRIPS against Bloods, Northern Mexicans against Southern Mexicans, Fresno Bulldogs against Pisas (Latinos from any country south of the border), or any combination thereof. All it takes is for one dumbass to throw a punch and your race is engulfed in a riot — and you must participate. If your race has *mandatory yard,* and you do not show up on the yard to fight with the group, you will be stigmatized as a coward. Then, after the riot is over, you will be either stabbed or rat-packed by other convicts of your race.

Over the years I have witnessed numerous race riots and have seen terrible things; prisoners being stabbed, prisoners being beaten unmercifully by a mob, and prisoners being shot by the guards. In one riot I saw a man get stabbed in the eye; in another, a guy had his head bashed in with a dumbbell. Once I fought in a race riot that pitted 270 Blacks against 50 Whites, and I was nearly shot on three separate occasions. Whenever a riot erupts, the fear of being maimed or even killed is palpable. You could also be charged with new crimes. The guards almost always videotape the riots, and anyone seen using a knife is charged with attempted murder, which carries a mandatory life sentence. At the minimum, the inmates involved in the riots will be disciplined and sent to the hole.

Following a race riot, the prison is locked down for an indefinite period of time. Sometimes lockdowns can last up to a year. During that time, the prisoners are trapped two to a cell, in grim eight-by-ten-foot chambers around the clock. The only exception is when the guards handcuff and physically escort the prisoner to the shower for five minutes every third day. All meals are served through a slot in the cell door. You are basically treated like an animal. The conditions are oppressive and the noise is maddening.

The cell doors are constructed out of mesh steal. As a result, you are subjected to every sound that emanates from the neighboring 25 cells: rap music blaring, unfathomably ignorant conversations, farting, defecating, flushing toilets, fistfights, crying, shouting, and screaming. Every morning the Mexican gang members conduct roll call, during which each homie in the entire building screams out his name. Then in the afternoon the same group conducts mandatory workouts with their leader yelling out instructions. This insanity is continuous throughout the day, every day. I saw many men lose their mind and get hauled off to the psychiatric security unit in four-point restraints. The prison during lockdown is itself a lunatic asylum. Imagine being confined to a small cell like that 24 hours a day, seven days a week, for months on end. If you choose to break the law, this is the future you can expect.

#5: *The Other Inmates*
Prison is filled with society's rejects. Most of the men are drug addicts who will do anything — lie, cheat, steal, deceive — to obtain drugs. Some convicts stink because they do not shower regularly. Some are loud and disrespectful. Many are mentally unstable. It's like being surrounded by a thousand hidden bombs; you never know what will set off one of them.

You do not get to choose your cellmate. The chances of you ending up with someone who shares your culture, values, or interests is about a thousand to one. Over the years I've been celled with some real freak shows. One convict named Ray laughed at the top of his lungs continuously for hours. Another, Sam, talked nonstop about all his fights, which I surmised was a defense mechanism. One dude from Tennessee cut the most God-awful farts all day, every day. It got so bad that I had to smuggle a surgical mask from the infirmary to prevent from getting sick. One of the worst cellmates I had made "pruno" once a week. Pruno is jailhouse wine that frequently makes people sick. When this guy got drunk, he was loud and obnoxious. He frequently made racial slurs to the Blacks who lived in the neighboring cell. This was a concern for me, because if the blacks attacked him, I would be obligated to come to his defense. If I didn't, then the other whites would send a "torpedo" — an armed attacker — to deal with me.

#4: Sexual Predators

I know its cliché, but rapes really do happen in prison. When I was at Tehachapi Prison, in the mountains above Bakersfield, I was on a yard with a homosexual rapist everyone called "Pincushion." The man had stab marks all over his body. In prison a confirmed rapist is a walking target. Anyone trying to build a reputation will take a whack at them. Because of this, Pincushion rarely left his cell.

Pincushion was kind of like a Venus flytrap, the plant that devours unsuspecting insects that land on its leaves. Pincushion would patiently wait for the administration to assign a handsome young man to his cell, and then he would attack him in the middle of the night. This happened to a 19-year-old kid when I was at Tehachapi. Pincushion tied the kid to his bunk, gagged him and then raped him repeatedly. Evidently this went on for several days before one of the guards looked into the cell during a routine count and saw that the kid was tied up. The convicts in the neighboring cells knew what was happening, but did nothing because telling is a stabbing offence. If you are young and you come to prison, there is a chance some creep like Pincushion could rape you.

#3: Access to Health Care

In December 2009, a panel of three federal judges ordered the State of California to release 40,000 inmates, because prison overcrowding had caused deplorable, unconstitutional health care conditions. Testimony from the trial revealed that at least one inmate dies every week due to medical indifference. The delay in seeing a doctor at the institution where I was housed was six weeks. Imagine being really ill and having no access to medical care.

Access to expensive medical procedures is often blocked. Back in the mid-1990s I shattered my ankle playing basketball. The x-ray revealed that in addition to a break, there were a multitude of bone fragments. I was sent to see an orthopedic doctor at a hospital in the city. He recommended surgery and ordered an MRI. When the MRI results came back, the prison's chief medical officer determined that surgery was not necessary. The prison doctor didn't even give me a cast. I limped around on crutches for over a year before the ankle finally healed on its own. It still causes me pain from time to time.

Dental care may even be worse than the medical care. Most of the time the dentists won't provide fillings for cavities, because it's cheaper to pull teeth. A toothless convict is a common sight on the prison yard. The longer a convict has been in prison, the fewer teeth he probably will have. I once heard one con ask another to punch him in the mouth to knock out his two front teeth. The poor guy had just learned that in order to get partial false teeth, the prison rules required an inmate to have only five teeth in his mouth, and he had seven.

#2: The Loss of Your Freedom

You know the old saying, "You don't know how much you love something until you lose it." If you choose to break the law, you risk losing the precious gift of freedom — the freedom to choose what you want to do and when you want to do it. In prison you will be ordered around and told what to do in every moment of your existence. Sometimes you even lose the freedom to choose when you can use the bathroom, and you are not allowed to handle your business in private. When you go to take a crap, your cellmate will be sitting just a few feet away. If he isn't working with a full deck, he may even stare at you or try to spark up a conversation while you're on the pot.

The first ten years that I was incarcerated I was held in either the county jail or level-4 super-max facilities. The only things I ever saw were concrete walls and dirt grounds. Then I was transferred to R.J. Donovan prison in San Diego, which is a level-3 maximum security facility. I was exposed to grass and flowers and birds. I was able to see and touch and be in nature. I was also allowed to go outside in the evening. As I watched a magnificent sunset, I cried. Later, I admired a full moon and the brilliance of the stars, and I felt immense pain over all I had lost when I lost my freedom.

The worst loss of all is the freedom to spend time with the people you love. The loneliness you will feel in prison is more horrible than you can possibly imagine. I cannot count the number of nights I cried myself to sleep. Prisoners are allowed to visit with friends and family members in the prison visiting room on the weekends. Prior to receiving such a visit your loved ones will be subjected to a humiliating and torturous process where they must wait in line for up to four hours, and may be strip-searched, interrogated, or told to change clothes. Is such treatment necessary? Of course not. It's a deliberate policy the prison has adopted to deter visitors. Think about that. Think about how the choice to commit a crime will affect the people who care about you. Think about the pain you will cause your parents. Do you love your parents? Then don't make the choice to break the law, because your parents will blame themselves. They will think that they failed as parents. When you go to prison, your parents suffer in ways you cannot now imagine.

If one of your loved ones dies, you will not be allowed to attend the funeral. Even worse, you will be put on "suicide watch," meaning you will be isolated from the general population for 30 days. On suicide watch you are not allowed to use the telephone or have visits at a time when you need them the most.

#1: You May Never Get Out

When you are incarcerated, there is no guarantee you will ever be released. I am aware of numerous incidents where men were killed prior to their scheduled release date. One convict, with less than a week to do on his sentence, was on the yard when a riot broke out. He did the wise thing and moved away from the violence. However, a bullet fired by one of the guards ricocheted off a brick wall and hit him directly in the heart, and he died instantly.

Another man I know about holed up in his cell during the

final two weeks of his sentence to avoid any problems. Since he chose this course of action, he was unaware of the fact that the other cons were on a work strike and had set up a picket line at the work-change gate. On the day of his release he unknowingly crossed the picket line because he had to go through the work-change gate to be released. The men on the picket line wrongly assumed the inmate was challenging the work stoppage and beat him to death.

You can also catch a new case that adds time to your sentence. One parole violator who was only serving a six-month sentence was required to go on a mission with two other convicts to beat up a known snitch. The snitch suffered a broken neck and was partially paralyzed. The parole violator was charged, tried, and convicted of attempted murder, which carries a mandatory sentence of 15 years to life in state prison.

CHAPTER 3
The Dillion of South Central

In the mean streets of South Central Los Angeles, CRIP and Blood gang members distinguish themselves in two very different categories: bangers and dillions. A banger's activities are protective in nature. They fight with other gang members and defend their respective 'hoods. The term "dillion" is ghetto slang for hustler; their interests include whores, drug dealing, and robberies. Rodwick Johnson, aka Black, was a dillion of remarkable distinction. Black's preferred crime, which he described as "licks," was armed robbery. His MO was to assemble a crew of three or four dillions and plan a robbery in another city.

During the summer of 2005, Black received a phone call from an acquaintance named Baby Buddha, who resided in Seaside, a beach community in Monterey County, California. Baby Buddha's girlfriend, Cecile, worked as an assistant manager at Home Depot. Cecile revealed that the store's daily receipts were frequently in excess of $100,000 and that the store was vulnerable to being robbed shortly after closing time, which was 11:30 p.m.

Cecile's insider information inspired Black to action. For the Home Depot lick he recruited two other dillions from the neighborhood, Big Money and Little Shorty. Big Money was a short, conservative-looking, 34-year-old black man. Little Shorty was a 27-year-old, shit talkin' gangster who looked the part. He wore sagging jeans and a blue bandanna hanging out of his back pocket. He drove a classic gang vehicle, a '76 Monte Carlo with 26" steel rims. Both men liked to use drugs, party, and get freaky with the loose women from their neighborhood.

Black and Little Shorty entered the Home Depot at 11:00 p.m., a half-hour before closing. Big Money was the getaway driver. He was parked a block away from the store near a freeway on-ramp. Black and Little Shorty ducked into the bathroom and waited for the store to close. Then they crept up the stairwell and sneaked into the ceiling rafters. They waited there for 30 minutes. Cecile had informed Black that the safe in the accounting room would be open at exactly 12:00 midnight.

Black and his accomplice quietly made their way through the ceiling rafters to the accounting room, which was 30 feet away. They removed a panel of the flimsy ceiling sheet rock at the stroke of midnight. They jumped down from the ceiling and rolled Kung Fu style. Both men pulled out their pistols.

Nothing happened. No one was there. The manager and all of the money were gone. Black's timing was off. He and Little Shorty left through the back door. The alarm sounded when they opened the door, but Big Money was only a block away, and they escaped easily.

Black considered hitting the Home Depot again the next night. However, the next morning he spied a Bank of America that he surmised would be an easy lick. He made a change of plans.

Black scoped out the location on Freemont Street in downtown Seaside. He noticed that there was an apartment complex directly behind the bank. There was also a freeway on-ramp that was easily accessible from the apartment complex. The bank had a back door. Only a low chain link fence separated the bank from the apartment complex. It was a perfect spot to park the getaway car.

At 9:30 a.m. Black walked into the bank. He approached one of the tellers and handed her a $10 bill. "Could you exchange this for quarters, please?" he asked politely.

As the teller stacked the quarters on the counter, Black cased the interior of the bank. There were four tellers and one manager. There was only one security guard, a tall, skinny youngster who looked like he was barely out of high school. He didn't carry a gun, only mace and handcuffs. *Too easy*, Black thought. *Way too easy.*

At 12:00 noon Black reentered the Bank of America alone. This time he was dressed for the occasion — an armed bank robbery. He wore black jeans and a black hoodie sweatshirt and a black ski mask. The plan was for Black to secure the bank by himself, with his crime partners entering shortly thereafter.

"This is a bank robbery! I want everyone to lie flat on their stomachs," Black loudly announced as he brandished his pistol.

In addition to the six bank employees, Black counted nine customers. All but one quickly hit the deck. An elderly gentleman just stood there staring at Black. "This is like a scene out of a movie," he said, clearly in a state of shock.

"Lie down, old timer, before I bust a cap in yo goddamn wig."

The fire in Black's intense eyes snapped the old gent back to reality. He got down on his stomach like everyone else.

Black suddenly noticed that something was amiss. The security guard was not lying on the floor. He felt a surge of anxiety as his eyes frantically scanned the bank for the missing guard. Adrenaline coursed through Black's body as he quickly searched the premises.

The guard was not in the bank. Black wondered if he had fled through the back door. Black cracked the back door open and saw the guard leaning against the building. He was taking a smoke break.

"Get back in here, or I'll blow your fucking brains out," Black snarled.

"Yeah, right," the guard replied, thinking that someone was playing a prank on him. Then he turned to see the barrel of Black's gun pointed directly at his head. The man turned white and began to tremble.

"Don't make me shoot you," Black added.

The young security guard re-entered the bank. Black cuffed him, and then laid him down next to the other employees.

At that point, Big Money and Little Shorty entered the bank. They also wore all black clothes, gloves, and ski masks. They went directly to the tellers' cash drawers and began to empty them.

"Where is the manager?" Black demanded.

"I'm the manager." The trembling voice came from a middle-aged man lying face down on the floor.

"Get up and take me to the safe."

The manager rose to his feet and exclaimed, "I need the assistant manager. It takes two keys to open the safe."

"Who is the assistant manager?" Black announced.

31

"I am," a heavy set woman said, her voice cracking as fear enveloped her.

"Get movin', lady. I ain't got all day."

Black realized that this lick was taking way too long. Normally he was in and out in less than two minutes. If one of the tellers had hit the silent alarm that alerted the local police department, he was running out of time.

The two managers opened the safe, which looked like a file cabinet. The large vault in the back was not where they kept the money. As the safe door opened, Black saw that it was flush with cash. An irrepressible smile lit up his face. He could not help it. Rodwick Johnson simply loved money.

He pulled a pillowcase from behind his back. The pillow case was prepared with a square hanger. It popped open and Black filled it with hundreds, fifties, and twenties. He worked fast and furious.

The three men exited through the back door as they had planned. They hopped the fence and made it to the getaway car. Big Money quickly drove to the freeway.

It was a clean getaway.

The dillions of South Central holed up at Baby Buddha's place for a couple of hours. Baby Buddha hired a smoker (a crack addict) to burn the car. The take was $310,000. The dillions split the money evenly and went their separate ways. Mission accomplished.

Rodwick Johnson's childhood reads like a book titled *The Parents' Guide to Raising a Career Criminal.* Rodwick's mother, Linda, became pregnant with him at age 16, and it was the first time she'd ever had sex. Linda's own mother promptly kicked her out of the house. Linda moved in with her brother, Charles, who ultimately became the only male role model Rodwick ever respected. A year later she married a military man named Ted. They had four additional children — Lisa, Teddy, Randy, and Nancy — who were each born one year apart. Ted showed favoritism to his own children. One Christmas all of the children, except Rodwick, received bicycles as gifts. He was even forced to sleep in the garage. Beginning at a tender age, Rodwick felt like an outcast in his own home.

Linda abused Rodwick both physically and psychologically. She threw parties for soldiers who were going to Vietnam. Once the soldiers were drunk, she would announce that it was Rodwick's birthday, and he was forced to walk around with a hat collecting money. It wasn't Roderick's birthday, nor did he receive any money or presents for his participation in the scam. The seed of the hustler had been planted by the woman who had birthed him.

Linda had a "do as I say, not as I do" parental philosophy. She also had a foul mouth. Yet, when she overheard six-year-old Rodwick repeat her curse words while playing with his friends, she abused and humiliated him. She washed his mouth out with soap in front of all his friends.

Rodwick committed his first strong-armed robbery at age nine. He observed a classmate named Zachary Thomas walk into a store and purchase a bag of candy. When Zachary exited the store, Rodwick demanded, "Give me that candy or I will beat your ass." Zachary complied, but later that day his mother called the police. That night Linda beat Roderick with a hard plastic section of a Hot Wheels track.

Rodwick flunked the sixth grade and was held back a year. He felt stupid and inadequate. He started getting into fist fights at school. He was always in the principal's office. That was in the early '70s when school principals were allowed to paddle kids. Rodwick always received two spankings, one from the principal and another from his mother when he returned home. His mother's punishment was the only one he feared; Rodwick never knew what his mother would hit him with.

As Rodwick got older, Linda's punishment became increasingly violent. One time he stole a teacher's purse and got away with it. A girl named Boobie witnessed the theft and talked Rodwick into returning the purse. The whipping his mother gave him that night left significant scars, which are still visible 40 years later. She whipped his naked body with an extension cord.

Once, when Rodwick was in junior high school, his Aunt JoJo was babysitting him and his siblings. JoJo told the kids not to go anywhere, but the kids ignored what she had said. Rodwick took his younger brother with him to the store. On the way back home, JoJo caught them.

"Get your little black asses in the car," she screamed. The yelling continued as they drove back to the house. Rodwick mentally prepared himself for the inevitable whipping he'd receive when his mother returned. Once in the house, JoJo hit Rodwick on the head with a golf club. Blood splattered everywhere.

Rodwick snapped. He turned and punched JoJo in the face. Then he tackled her into a bookshelf and they fell together to the floor. Roderick jumped on top of his aunt and began to pummel her with a wild flurry of punches, the years of abuse venting out of him in torrents of anger and rage.

Bam! Something hit Rodwick on the back of the head. He turned to see his mother, who hit him again with the butt of a gun.

"Boy, you better get off my sister!" Linda screamed as she pistol-whipped her son.

That night Rodwick cried himself to sleep. He had tried to explain to his mother that JoJo hit him with a golf club and he was only defending himself, but she didn't care. He wondered why his mother hated and abused him so much. He often thought that it had something to do with his father, whom he had never met. Linda refused to tell Rodwick anything about his biological father. Roderick was a scared and confused little boy who was afraid of his own mother.

Young Rodwick enjoyed hanging out at a strip center known as "The Pit." It had a bar, a large liquor store, and a casino with a Vegas-style poker room tucked in the back. The Pit was where all the hustlers hung out. Rodwick liked shooting craps, playing cards, and hustling. One afternoon Linda's closest friend saw Rodwick at The Pit and informed his mother.

When Rodwick returned home, Linda smacked him hard across the face several times. However, this time her 12-year-old son didn't take it lying down. Rodwick blocked most of his mother's slaps and punches. She grabbed him and they began to wrestle. The struggle ended up in the kitchen. Linda grabbed a butcher knife. She was hitting and stabbing at Rodwick, using the knife like a belt. He was cut several times. Fortunately, Rodwick's Uncle Charles heard the commotion and pulled Linda away just in time before further damage could be done.

Rodwick's only reprieve from the tyrannical abuse of his mother came during the three glorious months when school let out for the summer and he was sent to his grandmother's house in Watts. Grandma's house was undisciplined and full of bad influences, such as Rodwick's aunts and uncles who were all drug addicts. Both of Rodwick's uncles were members of the CRIPS gang. Every kid in the neighborhood Rodwick's age was also a CRIP. For Rodwick, becoming a CRIP was a rite of passage. He would not have to be "jumped in" or face any other type of initiation. He was from the neighborhood; thus, he was automatically a CRIP. That's just the way it was.

With adolescence came mischief and crime. Rodwick hung out with a group of five kids who referred to themselves as the "Junior Misfits." Rodwick considered himself the mastermind of the group. He chose the street nickname "Black," which was the surname of his half brothers and sisters, because he craved a sense of belonging and he wanted to carve out his own identity.

Black and his band of Junior Misfits went on a crime spree. One of his favorite licks was to simply walk into an open 7/11, and while one of his crime partners would distract the clerk, Black would sneak into the back room and open the door. There his cohorts were waiting to steal as many cases of beer as they could carry. The boys enjoyed drinking Colt 45. When they were full, they sold the rest.

The neighborhood used car lot was closed on the weekends. On Friday nights the Junior Misfits would break the chains with bolt-cutters and *borrow* a car for the weekend. The key was always under the mat. The car was returned Sunday night. The lick went smoothly for about a month, then one evening Black's homeboy Thad wanted to impress a girl named Julia, so he allowed her to drive. Unfortunately, Julia was clueless behind the wheel and was swerving all over the road. A police officer pulled the kids over. They got busted, and the lick ran dry.

Black was 13 years old and had no prior juvenile record. A

juvenile court judge found him guilty of grand theft auto and the sentence was probation. His friend Thad was later shot and killed in a gang shootout.

The Junior Misfits loved committing burglaries. Nothing was off-limits to the young hoodlums. They burglarized schools and stole ice cream. They broke into homes and took TVs, stereo equipment, jewelry, and anything else that appeared to be valuable. The boys also did "snatch and runs" where they would enter a retail establishment, snatch something they wanted, and run like hell.

One night Black was out doing robberies with a Junior Misfit named "Deadman." Shortly after entering a house through the back window, Black realized that Deadman had not followed him. Moments later Black saw a cop in the back yard shining a flashlight and realized that his homeboy had made a break for it. Black headed for the front door where he saw another cop. The house was surrounded. Black was scared, and he started to tremble when he saw the cop pull out his handgun. One thought repeated in his mind, *Run, nigga', run!*

Black swung the front door open and ran straight at the cop. It wasn't planned. It just happened that way. When they collided, Black grabbed the gun. The police officer was momentarily stunned by the abrupt confrontation and lost his grip on the weapon. Black snatched it from him.

Black took off running through the neighborhood. The cops chased him for three blocks. He jumped over three fences, and then ducked for cover under a friend's house. He stayed in the hiding spot for so long that he eventually fell asleep. When he awoke the police officers were nowhere in sight.

Another night when Black and Deadman were doing a residential burglary, something even more frightening occurred. The kids approached the front door and rang the bell. When no one answered, they went around back to find a sliding glass window. Black used a rock to crack the glass. He reached through, flipped the latch, and raised the window. It was at that moment that he heard a voice inside the house say, "Goddamn it!"

BANG! A gun was fired at Black a second later. The bullet missed and the boys ran for their lives. Once they were certain the homeowner wasn't following them, they stopped in the park.

"That's it," Black announced to his crime partner. "I'm done."

"What?" Deadman questioned. "You quitin' the Junior Misfits?"

"Hell no," Black replied. "I just ain't doin' no more houses. I ain't giving up robbing. It's too much fun."

Black should have quit altogether that day, but he had become addicted to the thrill, the easy money, and the camaraderie of his homeboys.

For his next lick, Black and his longtime partner in crime, Tony Aaron, burglarized the McMahan furniture factory. They stole TVs and several black light velvet paintings, which were extremely popular during the 1970s. They got away with the crime. However, a week later a girl named Lori, who was a friend of Black's girlfriend, informed the police about the furniture factory caper. Tony Aaron was later killed while committing a bank robbery.

Black was 14 years old. The furniture factory robbery was his second criminal conviction. This time the judge sentenced him to a youth rehabilitation facility called Boy's Republic.

The thing Black liked best about Boy's Republic was that he escaped from his mother. The anxiety and fear that were always present while under his mother's roof subsided. He slept well and felt safe, similar to being at his grandmother's house during summer break. The youth rehabilitation center was strict and regimented. To Black that was a small price to pay for the peace of mind that came from escaping his mother's daily wrath.

Another positive aspect of Black's 11-month stay at Boy's Republic was the discovery that he was a gifted sprinter and football player. Following his release from youth detention, Black attended Seaside High School in Monterey and became a star athlete. He was the starting running back on the football team. On the track team he ran the 100 meter race and anchored the 440 relay team. He frequently finished first or second. Black had always been a fast runner. When he was younger, he used to taunt dogs and get them to chase him to increase his speed. Now, prior to his races, teammates would chant, "The police are coming! The police are coming!" for the same effect. He was fast, but he could never outrun his compulsion for hustling. Black's athletic promise was ransomed for cheap thrills and quick cash.

Black's passion for burglary was eventually rekindled. One day he took a crowbar into the empty locker room during P.E. He bashed the combination locks and ripped off the other students. He kept the things that he liked and sold everything else.

During the summers at his grandmother's house in Watts, Black continued to hang out with other juvenile delinquents. The teenage CRIP gang members were constantly looking for action. One afternoon Black and Deadman were shooting dice at Luther Park, which was a Blood neighborhood. Deadman caught one of their rivals using crooked dice. He choked the cheater out and took his money. Other Blood gang members were in the park that day, and Deadman and Black soon realized they were outnumbered. They ran to their car, but could not escape the park. The Bloods used their cars to block the exit. One of the Bloods reached out of his car window with a pistol and started shooting at Black and Deadman.

"Them nigga's got guns!" Deadman exclaimed as he and Black ducked down inside their car.

"So do we," Black said as he reached under the seat and pulled out a semi-automatic handgun. He peeked his head up momentarily to assess their enemies' position.

"What are you going to do?"

"Kill they asses," Black replied.

Black got out of the car and emptied the entire clip into the Blood gang members' car. No one shot back. To this day Black does not know whether he killed or wounded any of his rivals or whether they were simply out of ammunition. Black and Deadman escaped unscathed. As they drove back to their neighborhood, Black savored the moment of battle. He loved the danger and excitement associated with being a gangster.

Black was busted a third time following a snatch-and-run burglary at a retail shop called Freddy Fast Pants. This time he served two years in the California Youth Authority. He was 18 years old at the time of his release.

For his next act, the budding career criminal decided to

become a drug dealer. Two of his friends from Seaside High School, Frank and Raymond, fronted him some dope to get into the game.

Raymond introduced Black to his cousin, a 27-year-old woman named Caroline, who everybody called "Red" because of her flaming red hair. Black thought that Red was one of the finest sisters he had ever laid eyes on. She had a pretty face and a body for sin. Red was a PCP dealer out of Los Angeles. She had come to Seaside to drop off some sherm sticks. Black quickly learned that the term "sherm" was derived from Sherman cigarettes that had been dipped in PCP, a chemical compound that got people so high they referred to it as an elephant tranquilizer.

Black and Red were attracted to one another from the moment their eyes met. Red invited Black to come with her to Los Angeles, and he readily accepted the offer. She became Black's lover and his mentor. She taught him the fine art of making love to a woman and how to rise in the PCP game. She taught him how to dress like a man and impress women. Red was married to a man who was in prison, but he wasn't being released for another year. During that time Black lived in Red's house. It was one of the most thrilling years of his life. Red taught him hustler's the game on several levels.

Black's initial role in the PCP enterprise was as a deliveryman. He enjoyed meeting the customers, and found many of them to be fascinating characters. One of the coolest cats Black hooked up with was Mr. Wonderful. He was a pimp with 11 whores in his stable. He drove a '75 Fleetwood Brougham. It was a clean machine. Red soon bought one for Black.

One day Red asked Black, "Do you want to be a pimp?"

"Hell yes."

Then Red tested him by pretending to be his whore. The next day she gave him $300. The following day she gave him $225. Black smiled every time she gave him the money. On the third night Red brought home $75. Black accepted it without question, and she smacked him across the face.

Black grabbed her ass and asked, "What the fuck is wrong with you?"

"Nigga', if you are going to do it, do it right!" she asserted in an angry tone. Then she softened and explained, "The first night I brought you $300. That means my ass is capable of pulling down $300 or better every night. Ho's will take advantage if you are soft. You gotta keep 'em in line."

Black never forgot that lesson, or anything else he learned from Red. To teach Black the importance of "never use the drugs that you sell," she had him prepare a huge batch of sherm sticks. Black got so high off the PCP fumes that he started to cry. He had never been so high or felt so horrible his entire life. Once Red was certain that her boy had learned his lesson, she ran a tub of cold water and ordered Black to get in. She had him hold an ice pack against his testicles and drink a few glasses of milk. Black thought the remedy was bizarre.

"What the fuck?" he questioned as he staggered against the wall and wobbled into the tub.

"It will help you sober up and make you feel better, baby." Red said. "Just trust me."

Red introduced her protégé to all of the neighborhood's top players and hustlers. She and Black frequented the freebasing parties, and Black discovered that he relished smoking cocaine. During the late '70s and early '80s, freebasing was a status symbol. Only players with big money smoked cocaine.

One of the players, whose handle was Old Kat, took a shine to Black and taught him "The Hustler's Code of Ethics." He said, "Never let your emotions undermine your discipline. Think big and you will have it big. Always keep track of your money. Never use what you sell. Never take up a habit you cannot support. A Cadillac ain't nothing but a black man's dream and a poor man's car."

Red was the first woman Black had ever trusted. She made him feel wanted and special, and she gave him anything he asked for. One night he requested a three-way with another woman. Red made it happen. Although he never verbalized it, Black loved Red. It wasn't a romantic love; it was the kind of deep affection one feels for a true mentor.

One afternoon the cops raided Red's house. Fortunately for Black, his younger sister, Nancy, was staying at their grandmother's house for the summer. Only a few moments prior to the drug raid, Nancy had picked up Black because she wanted to introduce him to one of her friends. They were standing directly across the street when a half-dozen police cars came screaming around the corner. The cops snatched the bars off the windows and front door to gain entry. They tore the spot up. Nancy was frightened. She grabbed her brother so fiercely that she left a welt on the left side of his body. They watched the police cart Red off to jail. She was bailed out by friends later that day.

Black and Red had a lot of fun together, but when her husband's parole date rolled around, Black knew that it was time to shake the spot. He decided to take the PCP hustle on the road.

Black and Red's cousin, Raymond, went to Bakersfield, where they stayed in a motel for two months. Raymond knew the terrain well. In no time they set up shop in California Park, where all the Sherm-heads hung out. Word got around that they were selling the best sherm in town, and the money started rolling in. Black was pulling down $1,000 a day. His life had never been so good. He bought jewelry and wore the best threads money could buy. He snorted cocaine off the hood of his caddie; he dated numerous young ladies. Black was living the good life.

One night at a club, he hooked up with a gorgeous woman who had a twin sister. The twins' mother lived in Los Angeles. Black offered to drive them to L.A. He introduced the sister to Reggie, who was one of the original Junior Misfits, and had been one of Black's closest friends since junior high school.

Reggie and his crime partner Otis were planning to rob some German drug dealers and wanted to know if Black wanted in on the lick.

"Do you even have to ask?" Black questioned. There was good money to be made in the drug game, but Black preferred the danger and unparalleled excitement that he found only when committing a robbery.

Otis had been buying drugs from the Germans, so he set up the lick. Around 10:30 p.m. they drove to the Germans' stash house in the Hollywood Hills. They had no idea how many men were present in the house. Their plan was based solely on the element of surprise.

Otis knocked on the door while Black and Reggie waited

anxiously beside the house. When one of the Germans opened the door, the three gangsters bull-rushed him. Otis grabbed the guy and stuck a gun to his head. A second German was sitting on the couch watching TV. Reggie drew down on him, and the man threw his arms into the air. Otis put handcuffs on the two German drug dealers while Black went from room to room, searching the rest of the house. Black opened a bedroom door and found a third German pulling on his pants. The man lunged for his pistol, which was perched on a nightstand.

"No way," Black said, his pistol already drawn.

Black pressed the trigger but the gun didn't fire. It was jammed.

Black raced the German to the nightstand, but the man beat him to the gun.

BANG!

The German shot Black in the side. The bullet tore through his rib cage. Black got to the German before he could get another shot off. The two men fought for control of the gun.

Otis heard the shot and sprinted toward the room. He tackled the German and the gun went flying.

Black seized control of the gun. He pistol whipped the German into submission.

The robbery netted the gangsters nine pounds of marijuana, three pounds of cocaine, and $15,000 in cash. It wasn't worth the risk. Black had a bullet inside his body and he was bleeding profusely.

"Homie, we gotta get you to the hospital, stat!" Reggie said. He pressed a t-shirt to Black's wound in an attempt to stop the bleeding.

"Let's get the fuck out of here," Otis said. "One of the neighbors probably heard that shot."

As they sped away from the crime scene, Black noticed that the bleeding had slowed down to a trickle. He put cocaine on the wound to numb the pain. Then he snorted a huge line. The euphoria clouded his judgment.

"I ain't going to no hospital. The smell freaks me out."

"You trippin' my nigga'? That bullet got to come out or you could die." Reggie was concerned about his close friend.

Black refused. They went to the home of Reggie's sister, Jackie. For two days Black lay on Jackie's couch and continued to treat the wound with cocaine therapy. When he finally passed out, Jackie quietly took him to the hospital. Later she told the police he was a victim of a drive-by gang shooting.

Black was rushed into emergency surgery. He woke up in the hospital two days later, unaware of how he got there. There were tubes running in and out of his body. He felt so alone. Then Reggie and Red started making frequent visits. Black was in the hospital for three weeks. Despite the fact that Reggie contacted Black's family, Black's mother didn't visit him or even call to ask if he was okay. She did not care about him. As Black lay in the hospital bed, his psychological wounds resurfaced. Black thought about his father, who he desperately wanted to meet. There were so many questions he wanted to ask him: Where are you? Why did my mother keep you from me? Do you want me? Or more to the point, do you even know I exist? Do you know that I need you? Black had never had the opportunity to ask these questions.

Black stayed at Reggie's house until he fully regained his health. Reggie's gangster lifestyle concluded a year later when he was busted transporting two kilos of coke on an airplane. He served 10 years in a federal penitentiary. Upon his release, Reggie went straight. Today he owns his own barber shop.

Once he recovered from his injuries, Black returned to his life as a hustler. He started slinging China White heroine for his Uncle Kato. At first, he struggled to succeed in this new element of the hustler's game. Heroin addicts are clever and unscrupulous.

One time he was outfoxed by an addict named Joe Boy with a "dummy sack." Joe Boy asked Black for eight balloons, which cost a total of $200. Joe Boy turned to walk away, then stopped. He turned around and said, "Never mind, youngster. I don't need them." Black returned the money to Joe Boy. He realized later that Joe Boy had put the heroin in his pocket and returned a dummy sack which contained only baby-powder.

It didn't take Black long to learn the game. Within a few weeks he was making $1,000 a day, just as he had with the PCP. When Black was riding high, he was generous with his money. He brought his sisters down from Seaside and took them shopping for new clothes. He frequently stopped by his grandma's house to give his Aunt Pokey a fix.

Pokey was a heroin addict and a whore. Her room at grandma's house was known as a shooting gallery because addicts stopped by to shoot up and have sex with her.

One afternoon Black entered Pokey's room when her prostitute friend, Ethel, was there. Ethel had a split lip and her eye was black and swollen shut. She looked like someone had hit her in the face with a brick.

"Damn, bitch. What happened to you?" Black said to Ethel.

Those were the first words Black spoke to the woman who would one day bear his child.

Pokey then told Black that Ethel's pimp had beaten her up. Black was not a man of moral fortitude, but he hated weak-assed niggas who beat on women.

Moments later a car pulled up in front of the house. The driver honked the horn and yelled, "Ethel May, bring your ass out here."

Black told Ethel to stay put. He checked the clip on his pistol, took the safety off, and went outside to confront the pimp. "Nigga, get away from my grandmother's house."

"My bitch is in there. Tell Ethel May to get out here right now before I whup her ass again."

"That bitch don't belong to you anymore."

"Mother fucker, who is you talking to?" The pimp was irate.

"That bitch belongs to me now," Black stated.

"Youngster, you don't know what you're talking about."

"Nigga, I told you to get away from my grandmother's house," Black said as he reached behind his back and pulled out the 357 Magnum. He shot out all the windows in the pimp's car. The pimp never came around to grandmother's house again.

Black stopped Ethel from selling her body and put her to work selling dope. They started a romance and Ethel got pregnant. Shortly thereafter, they were both arrested in separate incidents for possession and the sale of heroin. Both were sent to prison. Black's son, Bruce, was born in prison.

Black reluctantly admits that he was a terrible,

irresponsible father. Though he and Ethel have always remained good friends, and he gave her money whenever he was high-siding, he was never the father his son needed. Black's life was a runaway train that was destined for self-destruction, and nothing could derail him from that appointed destiny.

Black's ruthless, gangster mentality was counter-balanced by an inner sense of nobility. Black hadn't actually been busted for possession or for selling heroin. The police had raided his grandmother's house and his Uncle Kato had been arrested. Kato had a long record and was facing significant prison time. Black had no prior adult record, so he rode the beef for his uncle. Black turned himself in and accepted a plea bargain of 18 months in prison. He was released 10 months later based on good time credits earned.

He returned to the China White hustle. Within six months he was arrested again under similar circumstances. Black's operation was based out of an Executive Inn motel room he shared with his girlfriend, Susan. One evening he received a call from an addict named Dot. She wanted to purchase eight spoons, which cost a total of $200. Black walked across the street to Denny's restaurant where he usually met his customers. Moments later his motel room was raided by two cops. Susan was in the room. Black did the right thing. He walked up to the motel room and saw that she was in cuffs.

"The dope is mine," Black said. "She has nothing to do with it."

Black accepted a plea bargain for two years in prison. At that time prison inmates could earn half-time credits, so he was paroled after serving one year.

When he was released from prison the second time, Black attempted to go straight. He got a job working for United Airlines doing baggage check-in. He met a beautiful woman named Priscilla, and they got married. Even though he did not have the abundance of cash he was accustomed to, Rodwick enjoyed his job and domestic lifestyle. That changed when his employer did a background check and learned that he had lied on his job application regarding his prison record. He was fired. When money got tight, Rodwick's hustler alter ego, Black, emerged.

Priscilla worked the midnight shift at the post office sorting mail. Black had a hunch that any boxes addressed to Hill Street — the jewelry district in Los Angeles — might be valuable. He persuaded Priscilla to test his theory. She stole two boxes. One contained 20 gold bullion, which Black sold to "Carlos the Fence" for $4,000 each. The other contained gold fillings and dental plates. Against Black's advice, Priscilla sold the dental plates to a pawn shop for $10,000 and a mink coat. The couple bought a new corvette and pimped out the house.

One night Priscilla opened a package containing uncut diamonds, but she was afraid to steal it. Black was not. He dressed up in postal workers' clothes and crept in the open warehouse dock doors. He found Priscilla, who gave him the box of uncut diamonds. The lick netted the couple $500,000. Over the next few months they continued the theft operation and their nest egg ballooned to $800,000.

Black stashed the cash in bank safety deposit boxes and safes he had installed at various family members' homes.

Black was high-siding again. He lavished family members with money and gifts. Then the vampires came out. Black's Uncle Kato and Aunt Pokey were the first to bite.

Black was so excited about the uncut diamond heist that he bragged to Kato about the lick. He took his uncle to the stash spot to give him some money. Later Kato doubled back and stole $150,000. Kato had been strung out on drugs since returning from the Vietnam War, where he had watched the demise of his entire platoon. Black was aware of his uncle's psychological wounds, but the theft was an unforgiveable act of treachery. He wanted to kill Kato, who immediately went into hiding. Black's grandmother talked him down. He traveled to the Bahamas for two weeks to cool off.

When Black returned to Los Angeles, his aunt Pokey made her play. Black had gone to his grandmother's house to give Pokey some drugs. He made the mistake of allowing his aunt to see that he was carrying a large amount of cash. Black used the bathroom, and when he came out, everyone was gone. He had left his 357 Magnum on the kitchen table and noticed that it was not in the same place. He checked the gun. All the bullets were gone.

Something wasn't right. Black's wife had dropped him off and wasn't expecting him to be ready for pick-up for several hours. He called Priscilla on her cell phone to come and pick him up.

"Baby, I just received a call from someone who said they had you and that they wanted $100,000." Priscilla was frightened.

"Fucking Pokey!" Black growled when he realized that his aunt was planning to have him kidnapped. "Come get me, quick!"

Fortunately for Black, his wife had gone to her mother's home, which was nearby. She picked him up just a few minutes later.

As they were driving away, Black watched a car pull up in front of his grandmother's house. Four thugs carrying pistols got out of the car and rushed inside. He looked on in complete disbelief. Black wanted to kill his aunt, but remembered the pain his grandmother had experienced over the Kato incident. Black loved this grandmother and wasn't going to put her through that trauma again. He went to Hawaii to cool off this time. Later in life, all four of Black's uncles and aunts died slow, horrible deaths from AIDS. All four were intravenous drug users.

Priscilla and Black lived the high life for a year and a half before the Feds busted them. The dental plates that Priscilla had sold to the pawn shop were engraved with serial numbers. Black had advised his wife against dealing with pawn shops, because they are required to record their customer's driver's license numbers. Both made plea bargains for three years in prison.

Priscilla was released from prison first and cheated on Black. When he found out that she had gotten pregnant by another man, he filed for divorce. Then he promptly went on another crime spree.

Black had acquired a taste for the big money associated with stealing jewelry. Since he was such a fast runner, he decided to revise the old snatch-and-run routine from his youth, targeting jewelry stores. Black recruited a young man named Skip to be his crime partner. Their first lick was a Cresson & Zale's jewelry store. The two men smashed the glass jewelry cases with rocks. They snatched as many Rolex watches, chains, and wedding rings as they could stuff into a pillow case in 60 seconds, and then ran like the wind.

It didn't take Black long to realize that there was a less risky way to rip off jewelry stores. The snatch and run was retired in favor of a new method Black called the "smash and grab." Black assembled a team of four criminals from the 'hood. They called themselves "The Rolex Crew." Their MO was to study the layout of large department stores, such as Macys. Their objective was to find stores where their jewelry department was located near a glass storefront facing the street. Smash-and-grab heists involved smashing the glass storefront after hours. Three Rolex crew members would then run into the store, smash open the glass jewelry cases, and grab as much jewelry as possible in 60 seconds. The fourth crew member was the getaway driver. Getting in and out in less than a minute was critical, because the police response time was usually about two minutes, depending on how close the police station was. The Rolex Crew went to Seattle and worked their way down the Pacific Coast. The month-long expedition netted Black $500,000 after the jewelry was sold to a fence.

Black had larceny in his blood. Despite his substantial cash reserves, Black continued to rob jewelry stores. The next lick went bad. It was an armed robbery in San Bernardino. The four-man Rolex Crew got away with a huge cache, but a Good Samaritan witnessed the robbery and followed the criminals. The Good Samaritan even watched them change cars. He called the police from a cell phone.

The cops rolled up behind the Rolex Crew and ordered them to pull over. Not a chance. They took off and a high-speed chase ensued. The getaway driver tried to lose them in a residential neighborhood, but crashed into a car.

The four criminals took off running in different directions. Black ran through an apartment complex and stumbled upon an idling car. He jumped in the driver's seat and hit the gas. As he exited the apartment complex, he passed the breathless cop who had been chasing him on foot. Black flipped off the police officer and laughed, because he was sure that he was going to get away.

In the sky a Channel 7 News helicopter was hovering overhead and videotaping the scene. The copter trained a spotlight on Black's stolen car, alerting a group of patrol cars to his whereabouts.

"Motherfuckers!" Black screamed as he pounded the steering wheel.

Black had seen high-speed chases on TV, and he knew the longer he was behind the wheel, the less chance he had to escape. He drove into another apartment complex, exited the car, and took off running. He seemingly evaded the chopper's spotlight and found a hiding place behind a dumpster.

Moments later several squad cars arrived, and he was off to the races on foot again with several cops in fast pursuit. Black lost his balance and fell in the middle of a four-lane street. He was exhausted. It was time to give up.

"Move, nigger, and I'll blow your head off," shouted a redneck cop who pointed a shotgun at Black.

Black was galvanized by the order. He jumped up and took off running again. The Channel 7 News helicopter was again shining the spotlight directly on him, and to this day Black is convinced that was the only reason he wasn't killed by the police that day. Another cop tackled him. The race was over. Black lost his freedom again.

Black was convicted of the robbery and sentenced to 12 years. During his incarceration, California passed the three-strikes initiative under which anyone convicted of three felonies would receive a 25-years-to-life sentence. Black knew several cons who received their third strike while in prison for petty crimes, including possession of one gram of heroin, possession of a hypodermic needle with trace amounts of methamphetamine, a fist fight that resulted in no more than a split lip, and even misdemeanor pot possession. Prosecutors all across the state were seizing the opportunity to throw away the key on repeat offenders. Black put his neck in the noose by getting caught with a small marijuana joint. He was fortunate to be offered a four-year plea bargain. Altogether, he served just less than nine years for the two crimes. It was his first long stint in the Big House and it was enough to convince him to give up the hustler lifestyle...for four months.

While he was incarcerated, Black married a woman named Shirley. When he was released on parole, he and Shirley rented a house together. He was hired as a forklift operator, but his employment lasted only a couple of months. Once again he was fired when a background check revealed that he had lied about his prison record on his job application. Money problems ensued. Black got a case of the "fuck its."

It was at this time that Baby Buddha called Black and relayed the insider information concerning the Home Depot. Black was aware that he was facing a life sentence under the draconian Three Strikes Law, but he said, "Fuck it. I ain't living like this. I can put down one more lick to get me through until I get another job." That lick was the robbery of the Bank of America in Seaside mentioned at the beginning of this chapter. Although he got away with the crime at the time, three months later his crime partner Little Shorty was arrested for a parole violation. For reasons still unclear to Black, Little Shorty told the police everything about the bank robbery. The police raided their home and discovered Black's safety deposit boxes. Shirley had told a girlfriend about the lick, and she agreed to testify. Other witnesses put Black in Seaside at the time of the crime. The circumstantial evidence was over-whelming.

Black was facing 180-years to life in prison if he was convicted of the bank robbery. The prosecutor had an open and shut case, but he threw Black a lifeline. The prosecutor offered Black a plea of 40-years, of which he would have to do 85 percent, which was 34 years. Black was 45 years old when he signed the plea agreement. This means he will be 79 years of age when he finally becomes eligible for parole.

The theme of this book is the crime and lessons learned. For Rodwick Johnson, the learning of his life's lessons began when he participated in a prison self-help program called Amity. The Amity program is facilitated by drug counselors and revolves around inmate support groups. Inmates stand before the group, tell their stories, and receive instructions and support. Rodwick listened to the other inmates as they opened up, exposed their lives, and told their deepest, darkest secrets to the group. Some of the stories brought tears to Rodwick's eyes. He empathized with their pain, but soon grew to realize that the tears he was shedding were also a result of his own profound pain. Many of the prisoners had endured childhoods that were even more horrific than his own.

Rodwick found some men he could talk to about issues that had haunted him his entire life. It was a real support group. He learned that men need other men they can lean on and talk to about the difficulties of life. It helps to discuss life's pressures with someone who is sympathetic. We all need that, especially during times of trouble.

When Rodwick finally found the courage to tell his story about his abusive mother and dysfunctional aunts and uncles to the group, he received feedback that enabled him to understand why he had severe issues with authority. He discovered that as a child he had low self-esteem, that he was insecure, and that he was desperate for acceptance. As he probed deeper, Rodwick realized that the first time he ever felt a sense of belonging was with the Junior Misfits. His first true bonding experience with other human beings happened when he and his adolescent friends committed crimes. An examination of his criminal history reveals that he almost always had a crime partner. A successful robbery was invariably followed by a group celebration that revolved around booze and drugs. The only time he truly felt secure was when he had a lot of money. When he had money he was generous, and inevitably family members, friends, and women vied for his affection. He was constantly trying to purchase a form of love he had never known — self-love.

When I asked Rodwick how he wanted his story to conclude, he said these four words: "Mom, I forgive you."

This chapter finishes with a warning to anyone who thinks they can commit the crimes that Rodwick committed in the '70s and '80s and get off with a light sentence. The sentencing laws have changed dramatically. Just say "no" to drugs and committing crimes.

What Factors Draw People to Gangs?
- A sense of importance, acceptance and belonging
- Having power over others, strike terror and fear in others
- Self-rule, lawlessness
- Money, parties, sex
- Prefer to be victimizer than the victim, feel safe

CHAPTER 4
Blockbuster Bandits

Matt Maroki started shoplifting in junior high school. In the beginning, he stole candy from 7-11 and other convenience stores because he liked the excitement and thrill of doing something illegal. He got away with it every time. In high school, Matt shoplifted from clothing stores. It was easy; he would simply walk into a store wearing baggy clothes, select several outfits, and head for the changing room. Matt would try on all the different clothes and interact with the store's staff. He asked for their opinion regarding which outfit looked the best on him. When he exited the changing room, he wore the items he planned to steal under his baggy clothes. To divert attention, Matt always purchased something inexpensive, such as a pair of socks. He never got caught. Matt did not once consider the potential consequences of his shoplifting or the fact that he was planting dark seeds that would grow dangerously out of control.

The flashpoint in Matt's criminality was marijuana. One evening when Matt was 15 years old, he got stoned at the home of his neighbor, Cody Smith. Cody's 6'10" height and full beard gave one the impression he was a grown man. He wasn't. Cody was a 17-year-old high school senior. He was the center on the school's basketball team. Also present at Cody's house was Tony Barnes, a mischievous hillbilly from the Appalachian Mountains in eastern Kentucky. Everybody on the basketball team called Tony "Wildcat" because he was constantly yapping about the Kentucky Wildcats college basketball team. Wildcat was an 18-year-old senior point guard. Matt was the team's equipment manager and statistician. He hero-worshiped the two seniors and did whatever they asked him to do.

"Dude, this is some killer weed," Cody said. "Where'd you score it?"

"I stole it from a Bigfoot," the wisecracking Wildcat replied as he blew smoke rings into the air. "You want it back?"

"I got your Bigfoot right here, numbnuts," Cody fired back as he grabbed his crotch.

"Your momma's a Bigfoot. Your daddy's a Bigfoot. And that ugly sister of yours with the bushy unibrow across her forehead is definitely a Bigfoot. If any one of ya'll was caught rummaging through the garbage for food back home, you'd get shot. Ya'll are lucky you live in California where Bigfoots are on the endangered species list."

"This coming from the inbred, incestuous love child of a mother and father who are first cousins." Cody laughed.

"Ain't nothing wrong with cousins gittin' married," Wildcat teased. "The first time I had sex was with my stepsister."

"Hillbilly trailer trash!" Cody howled, and the room filled with marijuana induced laughter.

Matt loved the infantile, fun-loving interplay between the two older boys. He loved smoking pot and hanging out with his friends.

"Dude, I got fired from my job at the liquor store," Cody said.

"What happened?" Matt questioned.

"It was totally bogus. They accused me of stealing a case of vodka."

"Did you steal it?"

"Fuck no. I think it was that Indian turd, Deepak. He's the owner's precious son. Fucking asshole. I needed that job. My car needs new tires and new brakes and the insurance is already through the roof. When my parents find out, they'll take the car away."

"That's not going to work," Wildcat said. "It's a crappy Toyota, but we gotta have transportation. Are you sure Bigfoots need insurance?"

"Fucking Indian turds, they did me wrong, dude. I have the combination to the safe at the liquor store. I'd like to steal them blind."

"Maybe you should," Wildcat encouraged. "How much do you think is in the safe?"

"I'm not going to rip them off. I was just talking smack."

"Why not?" Wildcat pressed. "They screwed you over. They got it coming. I'll help you do it."

"I will, too," Matt joined the conversation. "Seriously, how much do you think is in the safe?"

"Quite a bit if we did it on a Sunday night. The owner puts the sales receipts from Friday, Saturday, and Sunday in the safe and doesn't go to the bank until Monday morning. There's at least $3,000 a day."

"Do you think it would be difficult to break in?" Wildcat continued to press for details. He was into using drugs and always short of cash.

"I don't think so. There are two back doors. One is just a screen gate. The other one is weak, but it has a metal latch with a lock on the inside. It might take some work, but I think we could get it open with some bolt cutters. The good thing is the entire back area is completely cut off and hidden by seven-foot-high brick walls."

Wildcat took control of the planning. It was decided that Cody and Matt would handle the break in. They would dress in black clothes and wear ski masks, because the liquor store had a security camera. They would purchase irregular sized shoes in case they left any shoe prints. Wildcat would be the getaway driver. He would remain in the car, which would be parked a block away.

The caper was planned for 3:00 a.m. The kids drove past the liquor store, which was located in San Fernando Valley. The street wasn't busy with traffic during the day, and in the middle of the night it was a ghost town. Their timing seemed to be perfect.

Cody and Matt made their way to the secluded area behind the store. They busted through the mesh screen door without difficulty. The main door was made out of metal, but it was flimsy and weak. The boys snipped away at it with the bolt cutters and bent the metal back with the crowbar until the inside latch was visible. They broke the inside latch with the bolt cutters. They threw their shoulders into the door and crashed through it. An alarm sounded off like the siren of a fire engine.

"Run!" Matt shrieked.

The two kids sprinted to the getaway car. Wildcat was

disappointed. He needed the money to settle his drug debts. When they were halfway home, he decided to turn around.

The kids drove past the liquor store. The alarm was still ringing, but it wasn't very loud. They drove to the gas station across the street. While they were pumping gas, the alarm stopped. They waited another 10 minutes, but the police never arrived.

The boys decided to proceed with their plan to rob the liquor store; however, this time Wildcat decided to park close enough so that he could see the front door and honk three short beeps if the cops showed up.

Cody and Matt hopped the back wall and went in through the wide open door. Matt filled a backpack with bottles of booze while Cody opened the safe. He took all of the cash and two pistols, a snub-nose 38 Special and chrome 357 Magnum. They were in and out in a flash.

The take from the liquor store burglary was $12,000, which the teenagers split evenly. Matt had his own money for the first time in his life. He enjoyed buying gifts for his siblings and girls he wanted to impress. He went to nightclubs, slipping the bouncers a $100 bill to allow him and his young friends entry. He partied all of the loot away in just five weeks.

When the money ran out, the three juvenile delinquents made the decision to commit an armed robbery. Wildcat's older brother worked at a Blockbuster movie rental store. Wildcat pressed him with questions concerning the store's management procedures, daily receipts, alarms, and safes. Then he formulated a step-by-step plan for the robbery. Wildcat was the mastermind and the getaway driver. Matt and Cody would execute the plan.

Blockbuster closed at 10:00 p.m. It took approximately 30 minutes for the store manager to tally the day's sales, which were kept in a safe in the back office. An additional employee vacuumed the floor and cleaned up. After completing their duties, the manager turned on the alarm. The two employees exited through the store's front door.

It was at this precise moment Cody and Matt arrived on the scene, wearing their black robbery clothes and ski masks.

"Get back in the store," Cody demanded as he pointed the 38 Special at the two employees.

"Oh my God!" exclaimed the store manager. She was a voluptuous, beautiful young woman with white-blonde hair and brilliant, aqua-colored eyes. "Please don't hurt me."

"We are not going to hurt you," Cody replied, waving the pistol in the direction of the manager's office. "We just want the money."

"Do you want me to frisk her?" Matt questioned with a husky voice, suddenly inspired by the manager's extraordinary good looks.

"Shut up, perve," Cody barked. "Stick to the plan."

The other employee was an overweight teenage boy with long hair and terrible acne. Matt thought he recognized the kid from school. "Let's go, fart-breath," Matt snarled. "Over there, in the aisle. Give me your car keys and your cell phone. Sit down and don't say anything." Matt saw the terror that registered in the young man's face. Holding the 357 Magnum, Matt felt powerful and in complete command of the situation. He wasn't the least bit afraid.

Cody took the manager to the office. "First, turn off the alarm."

The woman was so frightened that she got the code wrong three times before she was able to turn off the alarm.

"Now the safe," Cody ordered. "Don't do anything stupid."

Cody towered over the woman as she worked the combination lock back and forth. Her hands were trembling.

"Take a deep breath. It's going to be okay. I promise we won't hurt you," Cody reassured her.

Click. The safe opened.

"Put the money in this bag." He pulled out a black plastic garbage bag.

The manager quickly stuffed the money into the bag. Cody then brought her back to the front of the store and sat her next to the other employee.

"Did you get her cell phone and car keys?" Matt asked.

"I forgot."

"Get them while I go back in the office and cut the phone line."

The teenagers ran out of the store and found Wildcat, who

was parked a block away. They drove to Cody's house and went down to the basement to count the money.

"That was the craziest fucking thing I ever did in my life." Cody exclaimed. "I'm still shaking."

"You should have seen how fine the store manager was," Matt added. "She looked like a movie star."

"Numbnuts here asked if he could frisk her. What a pervert!"

Wildcat didn't hear a word they were saying. He was focused on counting the money. When he finished, he whistled loudly. "Are you ready for this? We got $24,925! Hell, yeah!"

Over the next four months the teenagers, who became known as the "Blockbuster Bandits," robbed six more Blockbuster movie rental shops all over the San Fernando Valley. The robberies were executed to perfection.

Everything went well with the robbery of the eighth Blockbuster store; however, when they were sprinting away from the store Matt and Cody were still wearing their ski masks and carrying their pistols. They ran directly past a police car driving in the opposite direction.

The cop slammed on the brakes. He exited his vehicle, pulled out his gun, and yelled, "Get on the ground, mother-fuckers!"

The kids kept running down the sidewalk. Then the cop screamed the words that stopped them cold: "Freeze...or I'll shoot!"

Cody and Matt were merely 50 yards away from the cop. The kids put down their weapons and sprawled flat on the pavement. Six additional police cars arrived moments later. The teenagers were handcuffed and taken to separate squad cars.

Wildcat was sitting in his car just 20 yards away. The cops pointed their guns and ordered him to get out of the car. For some unknown reason, Wildcat yelled, "I'm with them."

Later that night at the Sheriff's station, the boys confessed to all eight robberies of the Blockbuster stores. The next morning the boys were separated. Matt was taken to Juvenile Hall, where his personal nightmare began.

Matt soon discovered that Juvenile Hall is a violent place.

During the first two days he was held in a single cell for observation. A 17-year-old Mexican gang member named Demon came to Matt's cell and asked, "Who you running with?"

Matt studied Demon with the cautious curiosity of an astronaut who had just landed on a hostile, distant planet. Demon was short, but powerfully built. He was covered with sadistic tattoos. He had a spider-web tattoo on his neck, two teardrops below his eyes, the word "Fuck" on one eyelid and "Y.A." (Youth Authority) on the other. He exuded a menacing aura of danger. To Matt, Demon was an alien life form. He wanted nothing to do with him.

"I'm not running with anybody, I just got here."

"I know that, dickwad. What race are you?"

"I'm Persian."

"Persian, what the fuck is a Persian?"

"I was born in Afghanistan, but raised in California. My family is Christian."

"I didn't ask for your fucking sad sack life story. Are you running with us or the Maiate?"

"What's a Maiate?"

"You some kind of fucking moron? A Maiate is a nigger."

"I'm defiantly not with the Blacks." Matt's father was a racist who hated black people. He wasn't allowed to have black friends.

"Good. Then you'll run with us."

"Who is us?" Matt had no idea what the kid was talking about.

"You're a smart-ass punk. I'm going to kick your fucking ass the first night you get in the dorm," Demon steamed. He walked away from the cell.

Demon was true to his word. The first night after Matt was transferred from the observation cell to the general population, 96-man dorm, Demon attacked him while he was asleep. Demon cracked Matt in the head with a sock loaded with bars of soap.

Matt leaped out of his bunk, dazed and disoriented. He put up his fists, ready to fight. Before he could throw a punch, Demon took his legs out from under him with a sweeping leg kick. Demon took Matt to the ground, and pummeled him with a barrage of punches to the face. Matt tried to fight back, to get up, to get away, but he could not escape. Demon overpowered him and beat him unmercifully.

"Gimme your shoes, Camel Jockey," Demon snarled.

"My shoes?" Matt was confused. "Why?"

"Because I said, so punk." Demon punched Matt in the mouth and raise his fists to swing again.

"You can have the damn shoes," Matt said weakly. "I give up."

Matt removed his $150 Nike tennis shoes and handed them to the menacing gang member. Only then did he realize that 30 other Mexican kids were grouped around him.

"You're my bitch now, Camel Jockey," Demon said, laughing. He and his homeboys dispersed, leaving Matt battered and frightened.

The next morning Matt was cornered by a gargantuan black kid named "Knockout." The guy was 6'5" tall and 270 pounds of rippling muscle. Knockout was the dorm's Tyrannosaurus Rex; the undisputed alpha male. He had the heart of a bully and a thug's mentality.

"Why'd you let them Mexicans punk you for your shoes?"

Matt didn't know what to say to the giant black kid.

"What did they call you? Camel Jockey? You some kind of Arab?"

Matt found his voice. "I'm Persian. I'm not Arab, I'm a Christian. I was raised in the San Fernando Valley."

"That makes you an Other," Knockout explained. "The Others run with the Blacks."

"I'm not allowed to hang out with black kids. My father won't let me."

Matt knew he had just made a monumental mistake by the look on Knockout's face. His eyes smoldered with satanic fury.

"Racist!" Knockout yelled. He delivered a thunderous, open-handed blow to the side of Matt's head. The haymaker punch that followed crashed into Matt's face with the force of a sledgehammer. His nose exploded with blood as he crumbled to the ground.

Later that day, Matt watched as the Black and Mexican

gangs faced off over whose bitch Matt would be. Matt's $150 Nike tennis shoes suggested that he had money, which both gangs sought to control. The Blacks and Others had assembled on one side of the dorm, while the Mexicans and Whites gathered on the other. Knockout and Demon were arguing in between. Their poisonous hatred toward one another permeated the air. The atmosphere in the dormitory was electric.

Demon turned to his homeboys and said something in Spanish. The Mexican gang members circled like a pack of coyotes. Knockout threw the first punch; a glancing blow that sent Demon reeling. The Blacks and Others charged and the dorm room erupted in pandemonium. Matt's eyes were riveted on the race riot that was playing out before him.

"Get down!" a counselor screamed over the loudspeaker.

The brawl continued. Matt noticed what appeared to be the barrel of a gun pointing through one of the holes in the Plexiglas window of the observation room. Boom! A loud explosion was followed by hundreds of rubber bullets whizzing in all directions. Matt was hit three times before he realized that he needed to lie flat on the ground to avoid the ricocheting bullets. The bullets stung like the sting of a wasp and left huge welts on his skin. They also brought a swift conclusion to the race riot.

In the aftermath, Knockout and Demon reached a truce. They decided to split Matt's canteen money fifty-fifty. The youngsters were allowed to receive $40 per week from their visitors, which they could spend at the commissary or in vending machines. Matt allowed the gang members to extort him for one month. When Demon was transferred to the Y.A., Matt decided to make a stand. He returned from a visit and told Knockout and Gordo, Demon's replacement as shotcaller for the Mexicans, that his parents had cut him off financially. The gang leaders were not pleased with this new development.

"Then you no longer have protection," Gordo said. "Tonight after count time, your ass is mine." Gordo was eager to establish himself as top dog in the dorm. Matt would be an easy target.

Following the 10:00 p.m. count, the bunks in the back of the dorm were moved around to set up a small area where the boys would fight. The other kids moved to spots where they could watch the action.

Gordo equaled Matt's 5'7" height, but out-weighted him by more than 100 pounds. Gordo was fat, but he was also muscular and strong. Matt feared the 17-year-old gang member and didn't want to fight him. He wanted to run into the counselor's office and beg for help, but Matt did not choose that course of action. During his month-long stay in the dorm, Matt had learned that whatever happened in Juvenile Hall would follow him to the Y.A., which was where he would be sent following his court conviction and sentencing. Matt was determined not to be labeled a "rat" or a "coward." Matt was trembling all over as he clenched his fists and squared off with Gordo.

The Mexican kid threw the first punch. Matt blocked it and surprised everyone in the dorm, including himself, by throwing a counter-punch that landed squarely on Gordo's jaw. A collective, "Ohhh!" rippled through the dorm.

Gordo made a bull-like charge that drove Matt into the cinder-block wall. The fighters tumbled to the ground. Matt attempted to get up, but Gordo grabbed the back of his hair and pulled him to the floor. Gordo wrestled Matt into a corner and began to pound him on the head. Matt slipped away and finally made it to his feet. Gordo got up and the two boys squared off like boxers once again. Their tennis shoes squeaked as the boys circled one another and threw wild punches. Gordo rushed Matt once again, using his immense hulk to take him to the ground for the second time. Gordo put Matt in a headlock with his left arm and hit him in the face repeatedly with his right fist. Matt was powerless against the bigger kid. On instinct, Matt reached up and clawed at Gordo's face. When Matt's thumb poked Gordo in the eye, the fat kid screamed out and released him. Matt scrambled to his feet again. Gordo's vision was blurred. Matt seized the moment; he threw a left-right-left combination and all three punches landed squarely in Gordo's face.

"Kick his fucking ass, Camel Jockey!" Knockout screamed, unable to contain himself. Knockout hated Mexicans.

Gordo was exhausted and gasping for breath. Matt hit him three more times before Gordo made another bull-rush. He lunged for Matt's legs but dove too low. Matt side stepped the rush. Gordo stumbled and smacked his head into the wall. He rolled onto his back. Matt jumped on top of him, fists flailing wildly at Gordo's face.

Seconds later Matt was cracked on the back of the head by one of the other Mexican kids. The Mexican gang members descended on Matt like a storm of locusts. The onslaught was beyond belief. Matt curled into a fetal position with his arms wrapped around his head as the gangsters kicked him savagely. It was a brutal beat-down.

Boom!

A gunshot exploded in the dorm room, and the rubber bullets zinged around the room. All the juvenile delinquents hit the deck.

A Mexican kid who was on the ground next to Matt said, "Fight one bean, you gotta fight the whole burrito. You ain't never gonna win a fight against one of the homies."

Matt was confined to the Juvenile Hall dormitory for 16-months while his attorneys attempted to negotiate a plea bargain. During that time he was engaged in more than a dozen fist fights. Whenever a new kid came into the dorm, no matter what race he was, Matt was forced to fight with the kid. If Matt got the upper hand in the fight, a beat-down on Matt ensued. Matt's lone wolf status did not earn him any respect with the other teenagers.

The first plea bargain "deal" Matt was offered by the Los Angeles County prosecutor's office was 22 years. His attorney was ultimately able to negotiate a 13-year sentence, of which Matt would be required to serve 85 percent — 11 years. The kicker was that Matt agreed to two strikes, meaning that he would be facing a mandatory sentence of 25 years to life if he was ever convicted of another felony under the Three Strikes law. Cody was also sentenced to 13 years. Wildcat was only sentenced to five years because he didn't have a gun during the robberies.

Following his sentencing, Matt was transferred to the Y.A. detention facility where he would remain until the age of 18. At that time he would become an adult and would be moved to the state prison system for the remainder of his sentence.

Shortly after arriving at Y.A., Matt heard someone yell,

"Camel Jockey!" His heart sank into his stomach when he saw the face of his Juvenile Hall nemesis, Demon, glaring at him.

"Come here, Camel Jockey. I want to introduce you to someone."

Matt walked over to Demon, who was standing with five other Mexican gang members.

"This is Anaconda Jones," Demon said.

A tall, lanky kid of Cuban descent extended an inviting hand. Matt shook his hand. Jones squeezed it tightly, then jerked Matt toward him, wrapped his other arm around Matt's body, and held him against his chest. Matt struggled to get away as Jones whispered in his ear, "Chu wanna be my girlfriend?"

"Fuck you," Matt said as he pulled away.

"What do you think, Jones?" Demon asked.

"She's pretty. I want her."

"Fuck you," Matt repeated. "I ain't nobody's bitch."

"She's all yours." Demon said, laughing.

"Chu wanna be my girlfriend?" Jones asked again, this time with an exaggerated wink.

The gang kids busted up laughing.

"You come anywhere near me and I will slit your throat." As the words escaped Matt's mouth, he couldn't believe what he had just said or the fact that he meant every word.

Matt's response caused even more laughter.

Matt turned to walk away, but Jones grabbed his arm. "I'll stop by your cell after evening count. Make sure your cellie is gone so we can have some quality time together."

Matt pulled away and went directly to his cell. He busted open a razor and melted the two blades to a plastic spoon, fashioning a deadly weapon. His mind raced and anxiety filled his soul as Matt nervously awaited his confrontation with Anaconda Jones.

The cell doors at Y.A. had individual locks, and the inmates had their own keys. When the count cleared, Matt's cellmate went to the day room area where the inmates watched TV and played cards. Matt could have locked the door, but chose not to. He was ready to prove that he was not going to be anybody's bitch.

A few moments later, Jones was standing outside the door, peering through the bars. He looked both ways. Once he was certain that no counselors were watching, he entered Matt's cell.

Matt revealed his weapon. "I told you I was going to slit your throat. You ain't gonna rape me."

Jones put both of his hands up. "It ain't like that. I ain't no faggot. That was just a joke."

"Then what the fuck are you doing in my cell?"

"Demon told me that I had to beat you up. I don't even want to fight you."

Matt stood at the back of the cell. Seven feet separated the two boys. "This ain't going to be a fight. If you come one step closer, I'm going to cut you."

"Put the blade away, man. This is Kern County. If you cut me with that blade, the prosecutor's office will file attempted murder charges. Nobody uses weapons here."

"Fuck you," Matt said. "I'm doing what I have to do to protect myself. I know the law on self-defense. You are in my cell."

Jones backed out of the cell. He had no intention of getting cut by the crazy Camel Jockey kid.

The next day the counselors searched Matt's cell and found the make-shift weapon hidden in his mattress. Jones had snitched on him. Matt was taken to the hole, where he would be isolated from the general population for 30 days. The following morning he was taken to the counselor's office.

"Are you some kind of idiot?" asked counselor Ruiz, a conservative-looking, middle-aged Hispanic man with thick glasses. "Possession of a deadly weapon is a felony. If I submitted this to the D.A.'s office, they'd file charges against you in a heartbeat. That's strike three. 25-to-life means life. You want to spend the rest of your life behind bars?"

The impact of the counselor's words hit Matt like a tsunami. He started crying. His body shook with huge, uncontrollable sobs. He missed his mother and father and the kindness of his sisters. The pain of losing his freedom and pent-up fear exploded out of him in torrents of emotion.

"Look, Mathew," Ruiz explained. "You get one pass with

me. Only one. The Kern County D.A.'s office is serious about this Three Strikes law. None of my boys use weapons here. If you must handle your business, you do it with your fists. That's how it is here. Jones wasn't lying to you."

"Jones told?" Matt was shocked by the insinuation.

"Yes, he told me what happened because he didn't want to see you get a life sentence. Don't look so surprised. That shit about the so-called convict's code is a ridiculous fantasy. Somebody always tells. I know everything that goes on here. When you are released back into the general population, I don't want to hear about you calling Jones a rat. That boy did you a favor by coming to me. Now stop crying. You can't show these gang kids any weakness."

"Yes, sir," Matt said ending the conversation.

When Matt was released from the hole he entered "Gladiator School." For 30 consecutive days he was forced to fight a different kid. Matt's 18-month stay in Y.A. was even more violent than his time at Juvenile Hall.

When Matt arrived at Donovan State Prison as a fresh-faced 18-year-old, he was fortunate in that some older cons took him under their wing. Matt's counselor classified him as "White." He learned that in the adult prisons the Whites do not run with the Mexicans. On the outside Matt had always hung out with white kids. The Whites embraced Matt and he gave up his lone-wolf status.

As a new con on the yard, Matt was required to go on a mission shortly after his arrival. With two other convicts he was ordered to beat up a white man who had disrespected the Blacks by uttering the word "nigger" one too many times. Matt performed his mission admirably. Following a 30-day stint in the hole, Matt acclimated to life at Donovan. Unfortunately, Matt got too comfortable. He started purchasing large quantities of marijuana and getting stoned all the time.

Matt Maroki did not learn his lesson, which was that he made poor choices whenever he got stoned. The decision to burglarize the liquor store, which started his crime spree, was made when Matt and his friends were stoned. The other important lesson to be learned from Matt's story is that you must choose your friends wisely. If you choose to hang out with people who do drugs, commit crimes, or are involved in gangs, it can destroy your life. Matt's so-called friend, Wildcat, was a drug addict and the instigator of the crimes they committed.

Matt was recently moved to a lower level prison. He has five years remaining on his sentence. My fear for Matt is that he may never get out of prison, because he is unwilling to give up smoking pot. If he doesn't get caught using marijuana, he may make another poor choice when he is under the influence and not thinking clearly.

CHAPTER 5
Savage Sex – The Truth About Teenage Gangbanging

The CROP presentations are an all-day event where the kids sit at tables with the prisoners in the cafeteria setting. Between the talks there is *table time*, where the convicts work one-on-one with the youths to ascertain why they are getting into trouble and to counsel them away from criminal behavior. It was during one of these sessions that I had a disturbing conversation with Hanna, a surprisingly street-wise 14-year-old girl.

"My first week in high school, three separate boys asked me if I wanted to join their gang." Hanna said.

"What did you say to the boys?" I asked.

"I said, no," Hanna replied. "I know what they wanted."

"What did they want?"

"Sex. It's common knowledge that for a girl to join a gang she has to be *sexed* in."

"What exactly do you mean when you say 'sexed in'?" I pressed for details, still somewhat surprised by the ninth grader's nonchalant attitude toward the perverted gang initiation rites.

"It means that every boy in the gang gets to have sex with you, one after another."

"Do you know any girls at your school that have been sexed into a gang?"

"Lots. They do it because they think it will make them popular."

The phenomenon known as *gangbanging* is not an inner city myth. It's a real exploitation that is happening to high school and even junior high school aged girls all across America.

Why do young boys join gangs? And once they are in a gang, why do boys sometimes gangbang teenage girls? What has happened to young girls that makes them vulnerable to such sexual predators and agree to such degradation? What can parents do to prevent their children from becoming gang members or victims of sexual violence? The answers to these questions and more can be found within former CRIPS gang member Tim Harris' outrageous story.

Tim was born and raised in a lower middle-class neighborhood in Orange County, California. His parents divorced when he was only a year old. His father took his older siblings and moved to Ohio. Tim and his recently born baby brother, Ray, remained with their mother, Latisha, in Orange County.

Following the divorce, Latisha Harris spiraled into a dark depression from which she never recovered. Her husband's abandonment sabotaged her sense of morality. To make ends meet, Latisha turned to prostitution. She even turned tricks in her home with her young sons present.

Latisha was a neglectful parent. She frequently left Ray and Tim alone in the house. As a result, Child Protective Services took custody of the boys for their own protection. From age five through fourteen the boys were in and out of orphanages and foster care homes. Fortunately, Tim and Ray were always kept together. As a result, over the years they forged a strong bond and friendship.

Tim's happiest childhood memories are from the time he lived at the Albert Sutton House Orphanage, which was adjacent to Orange County Juvenile Hall. The orphanage was full of kids, so Tim always had someone to play with.

The foster homes were a completely different story. The boys' worst foster mother, Dorothy Masters, was abusive. Dorothy degraded Tim and Ray through the use of corporal punishment. Her favorite form of torture involved requiring the boys to kneel on the floor, upon which she had strewn uncooked beans and rice. This and other sadistic punishments lasted up to an hour, while Dorothy sat in a chair watching TV.

Dorothy worked during the day and attended school at

night. During the evenings Tim and Ray were left alone in the house with two other foster kids. Sixteen-year-old Monica was left in charge of the other three kids. Monica had been sexually molested numerous times throughout her childhood. Men had used and abused her. She also had physical deformities and a serious health problem that required her to use a colostomy bag. Monica was desperate for love and attention. Like so many victims of sexual abuse, Monica became a predator herself and Tim was her prey. After giving the other two kids a bath and putting them to bed, Monica would take ten-year-old Tim into her room and require him to have sex with her. Normally Monica was sweet and kind. Yet, she became angry when Tim's performance was inferior.

Monica's sexual molestation of Tim brought other terrible memories to light. At the age of four Tim had been abused by a teenage cousin, who made him rub his private parts between her legs.

When the boys became older, Dorothy began to take advantage of them. She woke them up at 4:00 a.m. and required them to pass out flyers for three hours before school every day. Yet, she failed to pay them for the work. Tim didn't take to the slave labor. He discarded the flyers into the garbage and went to his older sister Rachel's home, which was nearby.

Rachel and her other siblings had returned from Ohio the previous year. Tim and Ray were at Rachel's nearly every day, and they were always hungry. Rachel did not like the way her younger brothers were being treated by their foster parents. She went to the welfare department, where she requested, and was eventually awarded, custody of Tim and Ray.

Rachel owned a huge, five-bedroom house. The entire Harris clan resided there, including Rachel's four kids. There were a total of seven brothers and sisters, one of which had a young son. It was a house full of teenagers. Rachel did the best she could, but it was impossible to supervise everyone. Following several years of Dorothy's tyrannical oppression, Tim was free to do as he pleased most of the time.

Tim started smoking pot when he was 14 years old. At 15, he experimented with PCP. He didn't like it at first, but continued to use it because the so-called cool kids were doing it and he was seeking acceptance. To fit in with other neighborhood teenagers, partying became a way of life. Tim was always smoking pot, drinking, or doing PCP. Peer pressure was changing Tim for the worse.

Tim became increasingly angry. During tenth grade he was kicked out of three separate schools for acts of violence. At one school he was kicked out for fighting; at the second for starting a riot; and the third incident involved pushing a counselor. He stopped going to school because he was simply out of options.

He was only 15 years old at that time. He was too young to get a job, so he started hanging out at Jerome Park, which was inundated with pimps, hustlers, and drug dealers. Men in their twenties and thirties spent their days making drug deals, shooting dice, and managing whores. Most of these men drove nice cars, wore stylish clothes, and lived in expensive apartments. To Tim's young eyes, they were successful. He began to perceive these men as role models and envisioned himself as a hustler.

These thoughts were reinforced when Rachel started dating a man called "Shitty" who was a member of the Black Businessmen, which was like a black mafia during the 1970s. Shitty drove a new Cadillac that had the first car phone Tim had ever seen. He wore an enormous diamond ring that spelled out his name and covered three fingers. He lavished Rachel with money and gifts.

One day Shitty's business partner, Snowman, drove up to Rachel's house in a money-green Rolls Royce. It was the finest car Tim had ever seen. He was star-struck by Shitty and Snowman. Both men had extraordinary confidence and an aura of invincibility. Snowman popped the trunk on the Rolls, and Tim saw that it was completely filled with stacks of money and cocaine. At that moment Tim realized Shitty and Snowman were cocaine dealers...and he wanted to be one, too. He began fantasizing about becoming a man of power and influence like Snowman.

One night when Rachel was away, Tim and Ray broke into her room looking for money. They found something that would prove to be more valuable — pounds of cocaine. Rachel was holding Shitty's drug stash. Tim stole some of the coke and took it to Jerome Park to sell or trade for pot.

"That ain't no cocaine," one of the older cats said when Tim offered it for sale. "This young buck is trying to sell us baby powder."

"Try it," Tim said.

A pimp who had been shooting dice and eavesdropping on the conversation was suddenly curious. "I ain't passing up no free samples," he said as he licked the tip of his finger and pressed it into the coke Tim had spread out.

The pimp touched the coke to his tongue and declared, "Hot damn. My whole mouth just went numb. That there's bona fide 100 percent Peruvian Flake. How'd a little hoodlum like you come up on some pure cocaine?"

Tim had found an entrance into the world he coveted. He admired the men who hung out at Jerome Park, and he desperately wanted their acceptance. Tim endeared himself to the older homies by stealing coke from Shitty's stash and giving it to the neighborhood criminals. For the first time in his life Tim was the "Big Man." Some of the older homies took Tim under their wing. Tim was frequently asked to hold their guns or drugs, and he was paid handsomely for these services.

During this period of his life Tim was befriended by the Black Knights, a group of junior high school kids. The Black Knights were essentially a bicycle club consisting of 12- and 13-year-old boys who aspired to be a gang. The youngsters looked up to Tim, and he relished his own "Big Homie" status, which fulfilled his lifelong desire for belonging.

Tim enjoyed hanging out with the mischievous Black Knights. The boys rode their bikes around the 10-block neighborhood. They spent their days smoking pot, shoplifting, and chasing girls. One of the boys had a chicken coop in the back yard of his home, which they turned into a boxing ring. Fighting was a way of life for Tim and the Black Knights.

The boys were obsessed with bicycles. The local Schwinn stores displayed high performance aluminum bikes with awesome "motto mag" chrome rims. The young hoodlums devised ways to steal the bikes. A couple of the kids would distract the store owner by talking about their love of bikes and dreams of owning a store of their own some day. The boys offered to take out the trash and do other chores around the store. Once they worked the owner into the repair room, one of the youngsters would steal a bike from the showroom. The Black Knights were clever thieves. They would dumb down the flashy new bikes by sanding off the paint and repainting them with cheap K-Mart primer.

One afternoon Tim and his pal Bodi were kicking it outside Church's Chicken, eating lunch. They were wearing their gang clothes, with blue rags hanging from their back pockets. A police officer spotted them and asserted that Tim matched the description of a robbery suspect. The police officer began asking questions. Tim had not committed the robbery, and he ignored the cop's questions because he did not want to be harassed while eating lunch. Tim's blatant disrespect prompted the officer to arrest both Tim and Bodi.

After spending 20 days in the juvenile lock-up facility, Tim was released on his own recognizance. When his trial date arrived, the public defender who was assigned to represent Tim recommended that he accept a plea bargain for a 60-day sentence. He said the prosecutor had a witness who had picked Tim out of a line-up. If he took the case to trial and lost, Tim was facing three years in the Youth Authority. Despite the fact that he was factually innocent, Tim accepted the plea bargain. Tim later learned that the so-called witness was a Mexican man who lived directly across the street from his home. When speaking to the police about Tim, the Mexican man had only said, "This kid looks familiar."

When Tim and Bodi were brought before the judge, Tim confessed to the crime and exonerated his friend. Bodi was set free. People around the neighborhood knew that Tim was innocent, because the real culprit was well known. Bodi spread the word about Tim's act of selflessness. The incident elevated Tim's level of respect exponentially. He was viewed as a "down homie" — a man of high integrity.

After 30 days in juvenile hall, Tim was allowed a six-hour furlough. In his absence, the Black Knights had devised a plan to take over the neighborhood. They felt that the older gangsters who hung out at Jerome Park, the Santa Ana CRIPS, were soft. They wanted to start a new gang called the Waterloo CRIPS, and they asked Tim to be their leader.

The summer following Tim's release from juvenile hall, the Waterloo CRIPS initiated a series of assaults on the Santa Ana CRIPS. The older homies were repeatedly caught off guard and overwhelmed by the vicious youngsters.

A defining moment in Tim's gangster life occurred during a confrontation with Jerry Stokes at Jerome Park. Stokes was a beast, a huge ex-con with 22-inch arms. Stokes frequently got high on PCP and terrorized the younger kids in the neighborhood. Everybody was afraid of him, including Tim.

"Your momma's a bitch," Stokes barked at a boy named Bingo, who was one of Tim's younger homeboys.

Stokes was high on PCP. His eyes were on fire and his aura of insanity sent a chill through every member of the Waterloo CRIPS.

Bingo was a small 13-year-old boy. He wanted nothing to do with the PCP crazed brute, yet Stokes' blatant disrespect could not be ignored. Somebody had to do something. Bingo looked to Tim for guidance.

Tim was 15 years of age at the time. At six foot two inches tall, he stood eye to eye with Stokes. But Tim was rail thin. He was no match for the beast in a one-on-one fight. However, the Waterloo CRIPS fought as a pack, and all of Tim's homeboys were in the park that day.

Stokes focused his penetrating gaze on Bingo. He did not notice Tim reach into his back pocket for a pair of vice-grips. In a flash Tim cracked Stokes on the side of the head. The beast was momentarily stunned.

"Get him!" Bingo yelled.

Ten other Waterloo gang members attacked Stokes. There was no opportunity for the enormous man to regain his bearings. Like a pack of starving wolves attacking a giant grizzly bear, the young Waterloo CRIPS went at Stokes with intense fury. The big man fought back, occasionally landing a punch, but he was overwhelmed by the young gangsters. The Waterloo CRIPS took Stokes to the ground and kicked his head and nuts without mercy. When Stokes returned to his feet, he ran for his life. The boys chased him all over the neighborhood; some hit him with sticks and others threw bricks at him. Stokes never returned to Jerome Park.

Following the Stokes confrontation, word spread throughout the neighborhood that Tim and his Waterloo CRIP homeboys had valiantly defended the honor of Bingo's mother. Tim's influence and respect as a local gang leader reached new heights and it went to his head. He and his crew fought with rival gangs. The violence escalated from fist fights to gun fights and drive-by shootings. For his own protection Tim carried a gun at all times. At night he wore a trench coat to conceal his two sawed-off shotguns.

Tim's gang leader status brought him many perks. He and his homeboys did not wait in lines or pay admission at local parties. He was popular, he was handsome, and he was charismatic. Girls in the neighborhood threw themselves at him. Tim fell in love with a beautiful girl named Pasha. Yet, monogamy was a foreign concept to the 16-year-old charmer.

Pasha's parents were never home, and her house became the gang hangout. It was the place in the neighborhood where the teenagers partied; they drank, got high, and had sex. One night after Pasha had gone to sleep, Tim had sex in the garage with another girl named Christine.

One of the homies walked in and said, "Let me hit that."

At first Christine resisted, but Tim sweet-talked her into it. She was high and Tim was the leader of the gang. That night Christine had sex with four of the Waterloo CRIPS. It was the beginning of what would grow into a larger and increasingly more perverse lifestyle for Tim and his homeboys. The gangsters used drugs and booze to lower girls' inhibitions and have increasingly wilder sex with them. Then they discovered that the CRIPS from L.A. were pulling trains (numerous boys having sex with the same girl, one after another) on girls to initiate them into the gang. Tim and his crew followed their lead.

Tim became obsessed with seducing teenage girls. Nothing pleased him more than to bring a hot girl to his sex-crazed wolf pack. He would do whatever was required to lure them into the gangbanging initiation ritual. He found that girls with low self-esteem were the easiest targets. Tim's seduction revolved around his popularity and the party scene. He'd take new girls cruisin' around the neighborhood in his low-rider, and escort them to parties. He'd get them high and spend money on them. Once the girls were enamored on the lifestyle or the drugs, Tim would issue an ultimatum; they would be sexed into the gang or he would cut them off, it was up to them. Ninety percent of the girls went for it.

Tim's older brother, Marcus, lived in the nearby upscale Anaheim Hills neighborhood. He was married to a nurse who worked as a surgical assistant. Many of their friends were doctors who had teenage daughters. When Tim's younger brother, Ray, moved in with Marcus, an exciting new segment of girls became available. The Anaheim Hills girls had money, class, and exotic looks. At school Ray met white girls, mulatto girls, and Asian girls, all intrigued by the prospect of meeting Tim. His reputation as a good-looking, magnetic gang leader had spread to Anaheim Hills. Ray regaled the girls with stories of the wild happenings at Jerome Park, and their curiosity got the best of them.

Tim and Ray brought the girls Ray had met to Jerome Park. It was unlike anything the privileged girls had ever experienced. There were hundreds of people partying, gang fights, and sometimes even shootouts. The girls were awestruck by the spectacle. Talking the Anaheim Hills girls out of their clothes was not difficult. They were eager to be part of the Waterloo CRIPS' fascinating world, which seemed glamorous. It was also far away from the scornful eyes of their own puritanical parents. The girls could hang out with the alluring bad boys, experiment with drugs and sex, and not damage their good-girl reputations. Yet, these teenage girls had no idea what was in store for them. The gangbang initiation ritual was degrading, sordid, and sometimes violent. Many of the girls who participated were traumatized. The experience left psychological wounds on some that lasted a lifetime.

One such victim was Melinda Sanders. Melinda was a year younger than Tim. They had been friends since junior high school. Melinda and Tim had a lot in common. Both teenagers' mothers had been prostitutes, and they were both protective of their younger siblings. Tim viewed Melinda as a good girl. He considered himself to be her "Big Homie," and he frequently looked out for her best interests. Melinda trusted Tim and looked up to him. A turning point in their relationship occurred when Tim found out that Melinda was sexually active. Tim's deviant alter ego was unleashed from its restraints. Like the mythical werewolf, Tim's transformation from Melinda's protector to her victimizer was uncontrollable. Manipulating Melinda to participate in the perverse gang initiation ritual was not difficult. Despite the fact that Melinda was a white girl from a good neighborhood, she was attracted to tough guys. She liked doing PCP and Tim was a PCP dealer. She enjoyed attending parties with Tim and his crew because there was never a cover charge and the booze was free. She was a gang-groupie and she wanted to join.

The Waterloo CRIPS rented a nice hotel room for Melinda's big night. All that Melinda asked was for Tim to get her high on PCP beforehand. Tim didn't have any PCP so he bought some Quick Start Carburetor spray from an auto store and sprayed it on a joint. Tim never gave a second thought to what the dangerous chemicals would do to 15-year-old Melinda's still-forming brain cells. The only thing he cared about was delivering her to the wolf pack.

In the beginning Melinda only had sex with Tim, and then eight Waterloo CRIPS entered the hotel room. One after another the boys had intercourse with Melinda while the others watched, drank beer, smoked pot, or masturbated. Some of the teenagers had sex with Melinda two or three times. As the evening progressed, the gang members got increasingly out of control. They defiled Melinda by using a broomstick and a beer bottle on her.

The effect this degradation had on the young girl's psyche was devastating. She thought Tim cared about her. That he would allow the other boys to do such despicable things caused irreparable harm to Melinda. She was never the same after that terrible day in the hotel room. Melinda was a prostitute for the next three decades. Today she is afflicted with the AIDS virus and is dying a slow, horrible death.

Tim told himself that Melinda was enjoying herself that day, but deep down he knew better. The truth is that Tim didn't care about Melinda or any of the other girls he and his homeboys sexually abused. They were simply meat for the taking.

Denise Dixon was another girl whose life was ruined as a result of her association with the Waterloo CRIPS. Denise was two years older than Tim; she was the first girl Tim had sex with when he was 14 years old. Denise looked like Grace Jones with a Jheri curl. She was ugly, but she had a fabulous body. Denise loved Tim and his homeboys and they loved her, too. When they were younger, Denise was the only one who was old enough to drive. She had a car and she was always cruising with the Waterloo CRIPS. Denise began dating a boy from a rival gang. He became so jealous of her association with Tim and his crew that he murdered Denise by shooting her in the head.

Another girl named Joan, gangbanged by Tim and his crew, also became a prostitute. She was found dead, slumped over a garbage can, with her dress hiked up. Her neck was slit from one end to the other.

By his own admission Tim Harris was a monster who ruined many lives. His message to teenage girls is straightforward: "Stop hanging around with gang members! They will use and abuse you. If a boy offers you booze or drugs, be aware that he has an ulterior motive. What he is really looking to do is lower your inhibitions and have sex with you. Love isn't having sex. If a boy really loves you, then he will be willing to wait until you are at least 18 to have sex."

Tim Harris was never arrested or charged with any crimes related to the gangbanging incidents. However, he has spent a significant portion of his adult life behind bars. Between the ages of 18 and 35, Tim was convicted of numerous crimes including burglaries, robberies, and drug dealing. This part of Tim's story was omitted because these subjects were covered in other chapters. Like Tim's personal testimony at the CROP presentations, this chapter was devoted to the segment of Tim's life that he is most ashamed of — his *dirty nasty truth.*

In 1992 Tim was arrested on charges related to selling drugs. He was facing a life sentence in prison under California's

Three Strikes law. One night while Tim was in the Los Angeles County Jail awaiting trial, he broke down and began to cry. He did not want to spend the remainder of his life in prison. It was in this state of depression that Tim began to pray for God's help. Tim's prayers were answered when the district attorney offered him a plea bargain of 12 years, of which he would be required to serve 85 percent. Shortly thereafter, Tim dedicated his life to serving Jesus Christ and was later baptized, becoming a born again Christian. During the ensuing nine years, Tim studied the Bible diligently, attended church and Bible study regularly, became a deacon in the prison chapel, and worked to eliminate his character flaws. Tim's Christian faith has become stronger as the years have passed, as has his commitment to make amends for the atrocities of his youth. Tim is scheduled to be released from prison in 2012. His plan, which he has been working on for many years, is to develop a CROP program in Tennessee.

Tim frequently concluded his CROP testimonial by recounting the following true stories:

Fourteen-year old Cynthia Morris, a high school freshman, had a crush on Thad Baxter who was the quarterback on the school's football team. Thad told Cynthia that he would be her boyfriend if she had sex with him. Cynthia agreed. The night that they had sex, Cynthia was unaware of the fact that Thad's friends were hidden in the closet with a camcorder, videotaping everything. Thad posted the sex tape on the Internet. Every kid at the school saw it. Cynthia was degraded by kids who called her a "whore" or a "slut." She dropped out of school and became a drug addict.

A high school senior named Jill Rollins allowed a boy who she liked to take naked photos of her with his camera phone. The boy passed the photos around to other kids at their school. The harassment Jill endured from the students was so vicious that she committed suicide. Jill's family and friends were completely devastated.

A 13-year-old middle school student named Hope Taylor made the same mistake. The boy told Hope that he loved her and that the photos were only for him. He lied. Hope endured relentless bullying from other teenagers. Some of the kids at school formed an honor guard to protect Hope from the bullies, but they could not help her escape the psychological trauma. Hope also committed suicide. Like Jill, Hope's loved ones were crushed by her suicide.

This chapter concludes with important facts and messages for young girls and the boys who think about exploiting them:

- The trend of "Sex-ting" naked photos is a crime punishable by up to a year in a juvenile detention facility if you are a minor. It is serious time if you are over 18.
- It does not matter if you take the pictures yourself or someone takes the pictures of you. It is a crime.
- Those convicted of sex-ting have to register as a sex offender – for the ***Rest of Their Lives.***
- People who are sent to prison with any kind of sex crime — even sex-ting — are labeled as rapists and will be stabbed by the other convicts.
- Young men over the age of 18 who have sex with girls 17 or younger can be convicted of statutory rape. In prison, rape is rape. No one cares if you were 18 and she was 17.
- Boys should know that having sex with a girl and then telling all of your friends about it is not cool. Imagine if someone did that to your sister or your mother. Treat girls with the same respect you want for your own loved ones.
- Girls, stop and think about the consequences of your choices, especially the choice to accept alcohol or drugs from a boy. You never know what his ulterior motive might be or if the drink or joint has been spiked with something that could knock you out and make you vulnerable to sexual predators.
- Cherish your body; don't give it to just anyone. Love yourself first. Honor your mind by taking school seriously. Recognize and nurture your special qualities. Respect yourself. If you don't, get help.
- Reasons why girls are sex-ting include: They want to be popular; they do not feel they are attractive enough to attract boys; it's a way of expressing thoughts they are too shy to say in person; it's a way of having control over boys.
- Once girls start sex-ting they eventually feel obligated to have sex.

CHAPTER 6
The Party Animal

Jake Masterson was born in Duluth, Minnesota. Jake's parents divorced when he was six years of age. His father, Max, moved to San Diego and occupied an apartment in a beach community called Mission Beach. During the school year Jake lived with his mother in Minnesota, and during the summer he stayed with his dad, who lived one block from the beach. During the summer between the fourth and fifth grade, Max married a woman named Carolyn. Max asked Jake if he wanted to stay in California during the school year. Jake's passions were surfing and skateboarding, and he loved Mission Beach. Jake elected to live with his father, Carolyn, and his new stepbrother, Mike, who was four years older than Jake.

His mother was devastated by the decision, but there was nothing she could do. Shortly after beginning high school, Jake's family moved into the trendy Jamaican Court District of Mission Beach. The neighborhood was saturated with college kids, beach bums, and surf vagrants. It was a nonstop party scene.

The most infamous party house in the neighborhood was the Coral House, appropriately named because it was surrounded by a magnificent fake coral reef fence that looked like the bottom of the sea. The Coral House was inhabited by six musicians. Their band, "GC in the Lap of Luxury," was popular during the seventies for their mellow, instrumental surfer music. GC in the Lap of Luxury put on concerts in their front yard nearly every weekend. Hundreds of people came to hear them play and party at the Coral House.

GC, the band's leader, invited Jake to attend a Hawaiian luau party at the Coral House. There were hula dancers, girls passing out leis (flower necklaces), barbeque being cooked on outdoor grills, and an open bar. People were drinking, dancing, and having a wonderful time. Fourteen-year-old Jake was enchanted by the atmosphere and captivated by GC's carefree lifestyle. That evening he drank alcohol for the first time. He got drunk and discovered that he relished the feeling.

Jake idolized the band members, and they took him under their collective wing. The Coral House was located right on the boardwalk. It had a huge redwood deck and a Jacuzzi. After school, Jake hung out with the band members who taught him how to pick up tourist girls. They were his party animal mentors.

Alcohol flowed freely in Jamaica Court. Another one of Jake's neighbors, Bill, was a 25-year-old surfer who was also into the party scene. Bill enjoyed Jake's company and was more than happy to supply Jake and his friends with alcohol. Drinking, surfing, and partying were a way of life in Mission Beach. Jake admired the older surfers in the neighborhood and embraced their hedonistic lifestyle.

Toward the end of his freshman year in high school, Jake and a few of his surf buddies wanted to experiment with hashish. An older surfer dude, a long boarder named Tom, was known as a hash dealer. The kids had surfed with Tom on several occasions and had no problem talking Tom into selling them some hash. Jake found that he enjoyed getting high on hash and marijuana even more than getting drunk. By the time school began in the fall, Jake was smoking pot or hash nearly every day. He was even smoking before school and during the lunch hour. He was stoned all the time.

Jake's parents purchased a home in an inland community called Clairemont midway through his sophomore year in high school. At first Jake's father allowed him to continue attending Mission Bay High School. Yet, when Jake's grades tanked because he was high all the time, Max compelled him to transfer to Madison High School in Clairemont. Jake hated the new school. His self-image was that of a Mission Bay elitist. The surfer crowd maintained the opinion that inlanders were total scumbags. Jake and his pals referred to them as "Claire Monsters."

Max was acutely aware of Jake's holier-than-thou attitude. In an effort designed to teach his son humility, Max required Jake to get a job at Burger King. Jake felt that the work was demeaning and below him. He loathed the polyester, maroon-colored uniform.

It was an embarrassment for someone of Jake's stature.

"Get used to it," his father exclaimed. "With poor grades you cannot expect to get into a decent college or get a good job. This is what your life will be if you don't take school seriously."

Jake was later fired from Burger King for drawing a swastika on the wall with a grease pencil. Jake was not a skinhead or even a racist. He was just fascinated by the Nazis. When he was younger, Jake had thumbed through his grandfather's collection of Time Life books. He was enamored by the Germans and the story of Hitler's rise to power. Jake loved punk rock music; many of the bands he admired lionized the Nazis in their lyrics. Jake became a swastika fanatic. He drew them everywhere and even got a swastika tattoo on his leg.

Jake's experimentation with methamphetamines (speed) occurred shortly after his family moved to Clairemont. His next door neighbor, Jeremy, a high school senior, offered him a line.

"Isn't that stuff highly addictive?" Jake asked.

Jeremy replied, "No. It's fun. Just try it."

Jake snorted the line. Moments later he felt euphoric. It was the highest Jake had ever been. He enjoyed it…way too much.

Jake was a natural extrovert who never had trouble making friends, but that changed at Madison High School. For the first time in his young life Jake felt like an outsider. Yet, when he got high on speed, he felt more socially acceptable. Throughout eleventh grade he relied upon the drug frequently to elevate his spirits, and in no time he was addicted. Jake had a large, valuable baseball card collection that included prizes such as Willie McCovey and Pete Rose rookie cards. The treasured baseball card collection was ransomed to feed his out-of-control speed addiction.

During the summer between his junior and senior years in high school, Jake expanded his partying favors to include cocaine, LSD, and ecstasy. Much of his drug use occurred when he hung out with Brady, his closest friend and surfing pal. There was nothing that Jake and Brady loved more than to get high, go surfing, and then cruise the beach to pick up girls.

Max and Carolyn got divorced, which resulted in Max and Jake moving to Oakwood Condominiums in Pacific Beach. Oakwood was a luxurious singles complex near the beach. The condos had basketball courts, tennis courts, a billiards room, gym, sauna, Jacuzzi, and a pool. The resort environment suited Jake's elitist self-image and fueled his party animal persona. Jake was ecstatic to return to Mission Bay High School. He was also elated to be free from his oppressive stepmother, and so was his father. Max began to take regular weekend trips to Las Vegas. While he was gone, Jake threw parties in their condo. He was doing drugs every weekend, alternating between speed, cocaine, LSD, and ecstasy. During the school week he got stoned on pot nearly every day. When the weather was good, he ditched school and went surfing. Jake didn't care about school. All he wanted to do was get high, surf, and hook up with the babes he met at the beach. He was the fifth worst student in his senior class, with grades of four F's and two D's. He had to attend continuation school during the summer to receive his high school diploma.

Following his senior year of high school, Jake fell in with a group of sleazy beach junkies. He was doing meth or coke every day. He moved in with Eric, one of his surf buddies. It was a flophouse for drug addicts. Even Eric's mom was hooked on speed. Jake's rent was a few lines of speed or coke every now and then.

One night Jake had a bad trip on acid and his elitist ego was spun out of control. He told the people who lived in the flophouse that they were gross scumbags and trolls. Eric's mom kicked him out of the house. Jake wanted to return to his father's condo.

"You cannot live here," Max told him. "My girlfriend Tessa has moved in. She doesn't want to live in the same place as a drug addict."

"Drug addict." Jake repeated the words, but they did not register. "I'm not a drug addict."

"Son, you need to take a long look in the mirror. You need to see yourself for what you have become. You have a serious drug addiction. You're eighteen years old. It's time for you to grow up and become a man. You cannot live with me and Tessa."

The conversation hit Jake like a thunderbolt. His father had always been there for him and always loved him no matter what. Jake felt ashamed and abandoned. He dwelled on the words "drug addict" and came to the realization that his father was right; the partying had gotten way out of control. Instinctively, Jake knew what he had to do to overcome his addiction. He needed to get away from California. He needed to return to Minnesota, to his mother, and the safe confines of his grandfather's home. And that's exactly what he did.

"You look like you just escaped from a Nazi concentration camp," said Jake's nana upon seeing his gaunt face and emaciated body shortly after he arrived in Minnesota. The meth and cocaine had ravaged his once athletic physique and stolen his youthful good looks.

Jake stayed with his mother and grandparents for a month. He got clean and healthy. He made a personal commitment to completely give up hard drugs, although he still planned to drink and smoke pot occasionally.

Jake returned to San Diego. Within a week he had reconnected with Eric and was strung out on speed. To afford their drug habits, Jake and Eric robbed garages in the upscale La Jolla neighborhood. Eric had come up with what the teenagers thought was a clever scam. The boys would prowl through cars in the supermarket parking lot searching for garage door openers. They would steal the garage door opener and follow the car owner home. Then, in the middle of the night, they would return to the home and burglarize the garage. They would steal power tools, wet suits, surfboards, fishing gear — whatever they could find of value. Sometimes they would sneak into underground parking garages and use bolt cutters to break into storage bins. The plunder was either sold to pawn shops or swapped for drugs.

One night Eric and Jake were high on meth and doing "hot prowls," which is what they called breaking into garages while the residents were at home and sleeping. They came upon a beautiful home where the garage door was open. The teenagers parked a block away. They were disappointed to find that the garage was empty.

"Let's go in the house," Eric said, as he checked the door and discovered that it was not locked.

"That's crazy," Jake responded. His moral compass told him not to enter the dwelling, but he was strung out on speed and needed money to get more drugs.

The boys entered the house and slowly crept down a hallway. In one room Jake saw a man sleeping and froze. *What the hell am I doing in this person's house?* he thought.

Eric was several steps ahead of Jake. In a separate room he found two expensive mountain bikes. Quietly he motioned for Jake to join him. Both boys grabbed a bike and worked their way back down the hall. Jake lost his balance and bumped into the wall, making a noise he feared would wake the sleeping home owner. They stopped and waited. Hearing nothing, they started toward the door. Again Jake lost his balance and banged into the wall.

"Hey," the homeowner yelled as he awoke from his slumber and saw the prowlers.

"Oh shit," Eric exclaimed. He dropped the bike and broke for the door.

Jake dropped the bike he was stealing and followed Eric out of the house. The boys sprinted to Eric's car. As they sped away, Jake's heart was pounding wildly and his mind was racing.

He knew that breaking into people's homes was wrong, but he continued to do it anyway. Jake and Eric broke into three other garages that night, and soon the car was loaded with loot they could sell or trade for drugs. At around 6:00 a.m. as the sun was coming up, Jake realized that he was in Pacific Beach. He had just ripped off a home that was only a block away from the Oakwood condos. He was stealing from his own neighbors! The realization pulled him out of the drug-induced vortex into which he had fallen.

"Drop me off," he told Eric. "I'm done with this."

Jake turned to his father. He realized that he needed help to overcome his intense desire to use hard drugs all the time. Max responded by paying for his son to attend an outpatient drug therapy program offered by Kaiser. Within a week Jake abandoned the therapy and started using speed again. The parents of Jake's closest friend, Brady, stepped up next. They arranged for Jake to attend a 30-day in-patient program called Calvary Ranch. The Christian-based rehabilitation center's motto was, "Where God does the healing." Jake only lasted three days. When other patients started speaking in tongues, he freaked out and made a break for it. He walked five miles in uncomfortable cowboy boots straight to the beach, scored some dope, and got loaded.

One afternoon Jake was frying on acid when he had a bad trip. He hallucinated that demons were coming to nab him. The unpleasant experience reignited his desire to overcome the addiction to drugs. He was driving down Calvary Street when he spotted an Army recruitment office. The thought occurred to him that the Army might be exactly what he needed to finally get straight. He went in and spoke to the recruiter. Jake was high, so the recruiter's pitch about the travel opportunities the Army offered seemed fantastic and enticing. He had frequently dreamed of living in Germany. Jake told the recruiter, "I want to be a military policeman," and he signed up that day.

The night prior to Jake's scheduled departure for Fort McClain, Alabama, where he would go through basic training, his surfing buddies threw a party in his honor. He got drunk and snorted lines of coke all night long. He got so high that he didn't report on time. He missed his flight. The recruiter panicked. He called Jake's parents and tracked him down.

Eventually Jake sobered up and made it to Fort McClain. He hated the Army from the first day. Jake especially didn't like being around the other recruits and soldiers, who were from different ethnic backgrounds and areas of the country. He thought the black recruits were stupid, and he considered anyone with a southern accent a complete moron. His elitist complex resulted in numerous confrontations and fist fights. On the weekends he called his friends in San Diego and asked them to send drugs, but no one did. He hated the Army's regimented lifestyle. He was frequently late for scheduled activities. At night Jake would sneak out of the barracks and run across the base to purchase tobacco products. His record of insubordination grew so quickly that his sergeant recommended a psychological evaluation.

"What seems to be the problem, Jake?" Alice Barnes, the military psychologist, asked. "Why do you think you are having so much trouble adjusting to Army life?"

"It's the people. I've never been around people like this before."

"Like what?"

"Blacks and southern rednecks. This place is filled with the dregs of society. Where did all these ignorant people come from?"

"Do you think you are better than the other recruits?"

"Of course. I know I am."

The look on Jake's face left no doubt that he believed every word he had said. Barnes diagnosed Jake with "narcissistic personality disorder." He was immediately discharged from the military. Jake only lasted 56 days.

He took a bus back to San Diego. He couldn't wait to see the ocean and go surfing with his friends. When the bus stopped in Yuma, Arizona, he saw that one of the other passengers from the bus was skateboarding. Jake sparked up a conversation. The guy shared Jake's interest in punk rock music and skateboarding.

"Do you do meth?" the punk rocker asked, offering Jake a line.

Jake had been clean for 56 days. He was in phenomenal shape. He felt awesome physically — and he wanted to feel even better.

Jake only hesitated for a split second before responding, "Hell yeah." He was high for the remainder of the trip to San Diego.

Jake was fortunate in that one month prior to enlisting in the Army he met a beautiful college student named Elisa. When he returned to San Diego, they began a romance. Elisa was a good girl with ambition. She did not use drugs and she did not want Jake using them either. She was an excellent influence. Motivated by the first real love of his life, Jake got his act together. He attended college and got a job as a waiter at an upscale restaurant in the Catamaran Hotel.

Over the next two years Jake tried to stay straight. For the most part he remained sober during the week and partied with his friends on the weekends. Whenever he got high he cheated on Elisa.

Then, in one horrendous week Jake lost his job, his girlfriend, college, and his apartment. The run of bad fortune began when Brady offered Jake a line of coke. Once Jake got high, he didn't want to come down. He bought speed and started calling in sick at work. Jake fell back into his familiar pattern of getting loaded, surfing, and picking up girls on the beach. He lost touch with reality. Elisa went to Jake's house on Easter Sunday. She brought him a gift basket filled with chocolates and some new surf shorts. He was buzzed out of his mind and Elisa knew it.

"You are high on meth again, aren't you?" she demanded.

"What? No, I'm good."

"You don't even know that it's Easter. We had plans. You said that you were going to get me a special gift to celebrate our two-year anniversary."

Jake was fading in and out of consciousness. He had hardly slept all week. "I forgot."

"You are a loser," Elisa said. "I'm done with this; I'm breaking up with you."

Jake felt terrible after Elisa left. He wanted some coke. Brady suggested that they buy coke from a local dealer named Blake. Even though Brady and Jake were regular customers, Blake refused to sell coke to them, so they decided to get drunk. The alcohol only intensified Jake's desire to do coke. When they realized they had no other options to purchase the drugs they wanted, Brady and Jake decided to rob Blake.

They went to Blake's home and rang the door bell. Jake crouched below the peep hole holding a skateboard, and Brady stayed out of sight. When Blake opened the door, Jake clobbered him in the throat with the skateboard. Blake, high on downers, stumbled to the ground. Brady, who was a huge man, began to pummel Blake with a barrage of punches to the face. Blake made no attempt to fight back. He curled into a fetal position. While Brady was beating the crap out of Blake, Jake went to his bedroom dresser, where Blake kept his stash. Jake quickly found a large zip-lock bag full of coke. When the two surf-thugs left the house, Blake was still curled up with his eyes tightly closed. He was so stoned that he wasn't even aware who the attackers were.

Two weeks later Jake was accosted on the beach by Todd Bolt, a hard-core drug dealer who was known to be Blake's henchman.

"I heard through the grapevine that you and that punk Brady robbed Blake," Bolt said as he put a gun to Jake's head.

"No way, man," Jake lied. "I've never robbed anybody in my life."

Bolt stared intensely into Jake's eyes, trying to ascertain

whether Jake was telling the truth. All he saw was fear. "You are fucking with my money, punk."

"I swear it wasn't me." Jake was petrified by the gun and the look of insanity that was written on Bolt's face.

"If me and Blake find out it was you, I'm going to kill you and that shithead
Brady."

The confrontation with Todd Bolt frightened Jake and Brady. They both shaved their heads and began to wear rocker wigs. Jake and Brady got an apartment away from the beach because they feared retaliation. When the paranoia became too intense, Jake decided to move back to Minnesota.

Jake's return to the land of 1,000 lakes coincided with his uncle's wedding. The love and acceptance he felt around family members was healing. Jake obtained a job doing construction work with his grandfather. Within a month he started feeling healthy again. However, after two months the intense drug cravings returned. He missed the beach and the party animal lifestyle. Following a few phone calls to Brady to make sure the Todd Bolt threat had passed, he chose to return to San Diego. This time he had a plan.

Jake moved into a bachelor pad with some surfers he knew. He started a job waiting tables at a health food restaurant and returned to college. His plan was to become a firefighter. For a few months he maintained a lifestyle where he partied only on the weekends. That changed when he fell in love with Stacy Anton, a blonde bombshell who brought out Jake's inner party animal.

Stacy was drop-dead gorgeous. She had an extraordinary body and a voracious appetite for sex and drugs. Stacy's favorite things in life were snorting coke and having sex. She was the wildest sexual goddess Jake had ever encountered.

It was during this period of his life that Jake fell in with a group of sleazy punk rock surfers from North Mission Beach. The rag-tag bunch loved to party and fight. Jake and Stacy fit right in. Prior to hanging out with the group of 15 degenerate punk-rockers, Jake had only been in a couple of fist fights during high school and the military. Now he was fighting every weekend, and he discovered that he liked it. He was a scrapper. Stacy loved the excitement, and she was often an instigator. They would be at a party and Stacy would say something like, "That guy just grabbed my ass." Jake would start wailing on the dude, and then four or five other punk-rockers would join in the beat-down. Afterwards, Stacy would nurse Jake's wounds and shower him with affection and admiration. Their life together revolved around drugs, fighting, and having sex.

One evening after work, Jake returned home to the bachelor pad to find a dozen of his punk-rocker friends plotting to seek revenge on three college kids who had jumped a surfer named Fritz. Later, they cornered the college boys on the boardwalk and beat them down. Jake was arrested for the first time in his life and charged with assault with a deadly weapon. He spent three days in San Diego's George Bailey County Jail. *Reader Magazine* wrote a story about the incident, warning people to watch out for a white beach gang called the "Surf Nazis." Jake loved the Surf Nazis moniker, but he hated jail. It was the worst three days of his life. Fritz was later involved in a murder-robbery on a golf course. He was convicted of murder and sentenced to life in prison without the possibility of parole.

The article in *Reader Magazine* and the stint in jail forced Jake to take yet another hard look at his party animal lifestyle. Even though his punk-rocker surfer friends did not call themselves a gang, Jake realized that's exactly what they were. Jake did not want to be a gang member, and he surely didn't want to return to jail. It was horrible. Jake stopped hanging around with the Surf Nazis, but he was unwilling to give up drugs.

The worst night of his life followed a three-day run of heavy partying on speed and cocaine. When the well ran dry, he took two valiums to try to come down. It didn't work, so he turned to Vodka. That didn't work, either. Jake became agitated, as often happened when his body was over-amped from a speed run. Eventually, he said, "Fuck this," and went out to purchase more speed or cocaine. He ended up at Blake's, the coke dealer he and Brady had robbed the previous year. Blake never did figure out who had robbed him, and Jake became his customer again.

Blake invited Jake into his home. Yet, Jake immediately sensed that something was wrong when Blake asked, "What do you want?" in a hostile tone of voice.

"I just want to buy a gram of coke."

"You still owe me $250 for the eight-ball I sold you two months ago."

"I already paid you for that." Jake couldn't actually remember whether he'd settled the debt. He'd been up for three days and wasn't thinking clearly.

"No, you did not. I'm getting tired of fucking with you, man. You always pay late."

"C'mon Blake, I'm spun out right now." Jake reached into his pocket and pulled out a $100 bill. "All I want is a gram."

"No. I've got a policy. No new business until old business is settled." He grabbed the $100 bill. "You still owe me $150. Pay that and we can talk new business."

"That's bullshit dude, I don't even owe you any money."

"You know what, here is you're fucking hundred dollars." He threw the crumpled bill in Jake's face. "Get the fuck out of my house. We are done."

Jake picked up the money, trying to remember the eight-ball deal. Maybe he did owe Blake the money; he wasn't sure. All he knew was that he wasn't leaving without buying a gram of coke. His nerves were on edge. Blake was acting like a douche, but he still thought he could talk him into selling a gram of coke.

"Look, I thought I took care of that, but maybe I'm mistaken. I can't figure it out right now because my brain is scrambled eggs. Just sell me the gram right now and I'll square up with you on Friday when I get my paycheck."

"No, I ain't selling you shit. You are bad business. Get out of my house."

"C'mon Blake, I'm not leaving without that gram."

Blake shoved Jake toward the door. Jake snapped and threw a punch that landed squarely in Blake's face. Blake attempted to fight back; however, Jake overwhelmed him with a series of punches. Blake fell to the ground. Jake was panting like a rabid dog. He stopped momentarily, unsure how the fight even started.

"Get the fuck out of my house!" Blake screamed.

Suddenly, Jake recalled the confrontation with Todd Bolt;

then he remembered that Blake once shot and killed someone who tried to rob him only a few months before. *I'm a dead man,* Jake thought. In that moment he realized it was kill or be killed. He saw an iron skillet on the counter only a few feet away.

Jake grabbed the skillet and swung it like a madman at Blake's head. Blake blocked the first few blows with his arms. He screamed out in agony as the skillet cracked his forearm bones. Blake was on his back, kicking wildly at Jake in an attempt to ward him off. Jake continued to swing the skillet at Blake's head. CRACK! BAM! SPLAT! Three horrendous shots to the head split Blake's face wide open. Blood splattered in every direction. Blake attempted to crawl away. Jake slammed the skillet into the back of Blake's head. He crumpled to the floor. Jake continued to smash the cast iron skillet into Blake's crushed skull until he could do so no more. Blake was dead. Jake dropped the skillet and stood over Blake's lifeless body.

"What have I done?" Jake spoke to himself. "Jesus Christ. How did this happen?"

A moment later, Jake heard a knock on the front door.

"Oh, my God!"

The door opened. A woman Jake had never seen before walked into the house. She shut the door and turned to see Jake covered in blood, standing over Blake's motionless body.

"AAAAAAH!" the woman screamed at the top of her lungs.

Without thinking, Jake ran toward the woman. He grabbed a Vodka bottle from the counter and swung it toward her head. The woman was so shocked by the spectacle she had stepped into that she made no attempt to defend herself. The bottle crashed into the side of her head and she fell to the ground. Jake straddled her body and lifted the Vodka bottle over his head to strike her again.

"No, please..." were the last words the woman ever spoke.

Jake slammed the bottle into her cranium, and it shattered. Blood and Vodka spewed in every direction. The woman was knocked unconscious, but she wasn't yet dead.

Jake's eyes scanned the room for a weapon to finish her off. Nearby he saw a heavy clay pot with a plant in it. Jake lifted the heavy clay pot high off the ground. Then with savage force,

Jake crushed the clay pot onto the woman's head. It was a death blow.

Just like that, Jake Masterson — in one surreal moment of drug-induced insanity — murdered two people in cold blood.

Jake ransacked Blake's bedroom, finding coke, money, and a gun. Then he drove to Brady's house to clean himself up. Jake told Brady everything that happened. Later, Brady told a friend, who in turn told the police. Jake was arrested just 17 days after the murders occurred.

Since the crime was a double homicide in the commission of a robbery, the prosecutor initially sought the death penalty against Jake. However, the prosecutor considered the fact that Jake was out of his mind on drugs the night the crime occurred. The prosecutor also considered Jake's lifelong addiction problem and his numerous attempts to overcome his addiction. Jake was offered a plea bargain of 50 years to life for the two murder convictions. He had no choice but to accept the deal. Jake was just 21 years of age.

If we trace Jake's drug addiction to its source, we discover an important lesson to be learned: Choose your mentors wisely. When Jake was 14 years old, he idolized the party animal surfers who taught him how to party and pick up women. The two times Jake had succeeded in overcoming his drug addiction — when he went to Minnesota — he had completely changed his environment, changed his social circles, eliminated his access to drugs, and ensconced himself with family members who cared about his well-being. If you or someone you know is struggling with drug addiction, heed these insights. Finally, and more significantly, the lesson to be learned from Jake's story is that hard drugs can completely alter your personality and turn you into someone you do not want to be. Drugs transformed Jake Masterson from a fun-loving surfer into a cold blooded killer.

Another salient lesson to be learned from Jake's story is the perils of drug dealing. Blake had been robbed by drug addicts on numerous occasions. If you start dealing drugs, you will subject yourself to people who will do anything — even kill — to get high.

CHAPTER 7
Shootout on 18th Street

Gang members are not born in a vacuum. Invariably, something happens during adolescence that causes a kid to choose to join a gang. In this chapter I will tell you the heartbreaking story of ex-gang member Diego Jones, who is serving a sentence of 100 years to life for his a participation in a gang shootout. It is my great hope that Diego's story will deter kids from choosing the gang lifestyle and provide insight for the many parents who are currently unaware that their children are at risk of becoming casualties of America's gang epidemic.

When Diego was 15 years of age, no one would have guessed that he would join a gang. Diego was an honor student, a member of the Associate Student Body, and president of the school chess club. He was a smart kid who appeared to have a bright future. Yet, appearances can be deceiving. What nobody knew, especially not his parents, was that Diego was consumed with fear, anger, and rage.

Diego was raised in a gang-infested neighborhood in East Los Angeles. Several times he was jumped and beaten up by kids from a gang called "18th Street" on his way home from school. Diego also faced ridicule from his classmates because of his appearance. He had terrible acne and endured "zit face" remarks and teasing on a daily basis. He felt ugly and funny-looking. As a consequence, he was afraid to talk to girls.

One afternoon Diego was hanging out at Huntington Park, which was near his home. He observed several gang members and was captivated by their confidence and bravado. They drove boss low-rider cars, had a cool sense of style, and always appeared to be having a great time. He envied their air of camaraderie, the fact that they had respect, that nobody ever messed with them, and that they all had girlfriends. Diego recognized one of the kids named James, who had been on his soccer team when he was younger. He wondered if James would remember him and allow him to join their gang. Diego was tired of being a victim, and he was tired of being seen as a geek by his schoolmates.

It took Diego about a week to get up the nerve to talk to James. Diego approached him in the park and was relieved that James remembered him. Diego told James about the problem he was having with the 18th Street gang members, and asked what he thought he should do about it.

"The first thing that you need to do," James advised, "is avoid 18th Street. They are fucking with you because you are in their territory. The next thing you should do is start hanging out with some of the homies. Nobody is gonna fuck with you if you kick it with the homies from our 'hood."

That afternoon James introduced Diego to some of the other boys from his Huntington Park gang. They played a game of soccer, and afterwards Diego ask them straight out: "What do I have to do to join the gang?"

At first the other kids laughed because Diego was such a square. Yet, once they realized that he was serious, Chito, one of the older homies, said, "You have to prove to us that you are down for the neighborhood."

"How do I do that?" Diego asked.

"You fight," James said. Then he punched Diego right in the mouth. "What chu gonna do? Be a punk and run home to Mommy? Or are you going to man up and fight for your 'hood?"

The punch caught Diego completely off guard, but he immediately recognized this to be a moment of truth. He surprised himself and the Huntington Park gang members by taking off on James with a wild flurry of punches. When it became clear to the other gang members that Diego was winning the fight, they rushed to James' defense. All six homies began to pummel Diego, and when he fell to the ground, they kicked him without mercy.

It was the worst beating that Diego had ever endured, but when it was over he was a member of the Huntington Park gang. All he had to do to get in was to get beaten down and promise to protect their neighborhood. That evening a party was thrown in honor of Diego's initiation into the gang. There were drugs and booze, and Diego got high for the first time. When he confessed that he had never even kissed a girl, the big homies hired a prostitute to have sex with him.

At first Diego loved the gang lifestyle and everything that went with it. He hung out with the bad asses and got more respect. Diego and James, along with two other kids from the Huntington Park gang, beat up a boy who used to call Diego "crater face." From that day forward no one at school ever made fun of Diego because of his looks.

Diego had stored up intense anger and rage due to the verbal and physical attacks he had endured. With the support of his homeboys, he began to prey on weaker kids. The violence started small; they would beat up kids just to steal their bicycles or skateboards. When they got away with those crimes, they became more brazen. They fought with kids from other gangs and started carrying weapons. Diego never went anywhere without his switchblade knife. One night, Diego and three of his homeboys ambushed one of the 18th Street gang members who had previously jumped Diego. Diego stabbed the kid six times, and abandoned him on the street to die.

But…the boy from the 18th Street gang did not die. Just two weeks later he brought a whole carload of his homeboys to Huntington Park, seeking revenge. James' younger brother Tito was in the park that day with his girlfriend, Lola. Tito was not in the gang, but he frequently wore his brother's clothes because he thought they were cool. The 18th Street kids shot and killed Tito. Then, they gang raped his 14-year-old girlfriend. Lola survived the savage attack and later told James that all of the boys had 18th Street tattoos.

James, Diego, and another Huntington Park gang member named Raffa, went looking for the culprits. Diego was driving the car that night. They cruised up and down 18th Street searching for their enemies. All three boys had guns. They did not see anyone on the streets during their first couple of passes—then they spotted two kids who flashed their gang signs at them. James recognized that they were their rivals. He leaned out the passenger's side window and opened fire, but he missed both of the kids as they ducked behind a red Chevy truck.

Diego pressed the accelerator to the floor. He wanted to get the hell out of there, but James was not having it. When they reached the end of the street, James instructed Diego to turn around. "I'm gonna kill those punks for what they did to Tito!" he exclaimed, his eyes fixed on the red Chevy.

Diego was more frightened than he had ever been. He did not want to drive back down 18th Street, but he knew better than to challenge James. He did not want to be branded as a coward, so he flipped a U-turn.

Diego turned off the car's lights and drove slowly. James leaned out of the passenger's side window brandishing his eight millimeter gun, and Raffa did the same at the rear seat window. Raffa did not say a word as he checked the clip of his handgun. All of the street lights had been busted long ago. It was dark and eerie, and Diego felt his hands beginning to tremble. His heart beat wildly as he secretly hoped the two rival gang members had disappeared into one of the nearby houses.

"Did you see that?" James said to his compadres as he spied a shadowy figure running across the street, then duck behind an SUV. "Was that one of them?"

"I think so," Raffa said as he shifted across the back seat to position himself at the other window.

"I didn't see anything," Diego said. "What if they've got guns, too?"

"Fuck it," James said. "We're gonna kill those punks. Let's go, man! Let's get this shit over with and get the fuck out of here."

Diego pressed his foot on the accelerator and slowly inched the car up the street. A dark figure emerged from the side of the SUV and started shooting at them...*POW, POW, POW!* The bullets bounced off the side of their car. A moment later someone else started shooting from behind the red Chevy truck on the other side of the street.

"Oh, fuck!" James exclaimed as he fell back from the window. "He shot me!"

Diego turned and saw that half of James' shoulder had been blown off. Blood was everywhere. "Jesus!"

Diego punched the accelerator, trying to escape the assault. As he passed the SUV, more shots rang out and Diego caught one in the forearm. He lost control of the car, and it crashed into a telephone pole. All three boys ducked down as the shots continued. Bullets were whizzing all around them. A bullet shattered the back window and another exploded the rear view mirror. A large shard of glasses hit Diego in the cheek, tearing off a huge piece of flesh. He screamed out in pain from both wounds. Panic coursed through every fiber of his body.

"They got us in crossfire," Raffa exclaimed. "Don't put your head up."

"Take my gun," James said, handing it to Diego.

All of a sudden the shooting stopped. Raffa peeked his head up and saw one of the 18th Street boys reloading his gun. He quickly leaned out the window and fired a single shot. *Bang!* He hit the rival square in the chest and the boy collapsed.

Inexplicably, the other 18th Street gang member ran across the street to his fallen homeboy. "Flacco, noooo!" he screamed, realizing that Flacco was dead. The boy rose to his feet and faced the Huntington Park kids. "You killed my brother!" he yelled. Then he ran toward the car, firing his gun in a maniacal furry.

Raffa unloaded an entire clip at the kid before he finally fell to the ground and died. An autopsy later revealed that the boy was shot 14 times.

Diego turned the ignition key and felt an intense wave of relief when the car started. He fled the scene with the sound of police sirens blaring in the distance.

Diego drove straight to the home of one of their older homeboys named Marko, hoping that he would know how to treat their wounds. Diego's forearm wasn't too bad. The bullet had gone through the muscle without hitting the bone. Marko dressed the wound and said that Diego would be all right.

James's shoulder injury was for more serious. A sizeable chunk of his shoulder was gone and they could not stop the bleeding. James faded in and out of consciousness. Diego and Raffa were afraid he was going to die, and they decided to take him to the hospital.

Marko gave a simple instruction to James before they left. "Don't tell. Hold your mud, homie."

"You know I'm better than that," James replied.

He wasn't. Diego dropped James off in front of the

hospital, where he was treated and then promptly arrested. Within an hour he cut a deal to testify and turn State's evidence against both Raffa and Diego. Both boys were arrested at Marko's home shortly thereafter. They had not even disposed of the murder weapons.

The story that James told the police was a complete fabrication. He explained that he was driving the car that night, and that he and his friends were out cruising to meet girls when they were ambushed. He said that only Diego and Raffa had guns. Marko also cut a deal to testify, and he corroborated James' story. It was clear to Diego that the Los Angeles County prosecutors had coached both boys, and there was nothing Diego could do about it. His fingerprints were all over the gun that James had handed him.

Diego was charged with two counts of first degree murder. Even though he was only 16 years old at the time of the crime, he was tried as an adult. Diego was convicted of both murders and sentenced to 100 years to life in state prison. He received a 25-year to life sentence for each murder, and two additional 25-year enhancements for using a gun under a new law that was enacted specifically to punish gang members. He was destined to spend the rest of his life behind bars.

Diego's parents used their entire life savings to hire an attorney to defend him. They were also terrorized by the 18th Street gang members, who slashed the tires of their car and shot out all of the windows in their home. They were forced to move from the Los Angeles area out of fear of retribution. Diego loved his parents and was deeply ashamed of the pain and suffering he had caused them.

Several members of both victims' families testified during the sentencing phase of Diego's trial. There were mothers, fathers, brothers, sisters, cousins, aunts, and uncles. Each cried when they spoke of losing their loved ones. Diego felt like a scumbag. He could not believe how many people he had hurt. Never once had he considered the pain of the 18th Street gang members' families.

The primary lesson to be learned from Diego's story is this: Don't join a gang, because you will create misery for yourself, for others, and for those who love you. This chapter concludes with five things every gangster needs to know:

#1 Understand the law of "conspiracy to commit murder": The jury instructions for conspiracy state: "You are guilty of every crime committed by your co-conspirators, even if the crime was not intended as part of the agreed upon objective and even if you were not present during the commission of the crime." One CROP member named Steve drove four of his homeboys to the home of Tony, a rival gang member. Steve waited in the car while his four homeboys went inside to kick Tony's ass. During the beat-down, Tony fell violently to the ground, hitting his head. Tony died instantly. Steve was tried and convicted of conspiracy to commit murder and given the mandatory sentence of 25 years to life in state prison. Steve was only 16 years of age at the time.

#2 Understand the law of "attempted murder": The law of attempted murder carries the mandatory sentence of 15 years to life. If you get involved in a shootout, even if no one gets shot, you can be charged with attempted murder. One CROP member was involved in a shootout where a rival gang member was shot in the butt, but not badly hurt. Despite the fact that he was not the actual shooter, the CROP member was tried and convicted of attempted murder and sentenced to 15 years to life in prison.

#3 Life means life for active gang members: The 15 years to life and 25 years to life sentences described above are known as indeterminate sentences. A prisoner with an indeterminate sentence may only be released from prison if he is found to be "suitable for parole" by the Board of Parole Hearings. An active gang member will never be found suitable for parole, because gang members are considered to be a risk to public safety. Thus, life means life for gang members.

#4 Your homies will rat on you: When several gang members are involved in a crime, prosecutors typically offer immunity to one gang member who agrees to testify against the others. You are a complete idiot if you believe your homies will do life in prison to prove their loyalty to you. Someone always tells. Prosecutors will even cut a deal with a murderer to gain multiple convictions. That is what happened in Steve's case, described above (#1). When Steve refused to testify, the prosecutor enticed one of the killers to testify against the others.

#5 When you join a gang, your family members will suffer:

I know a gang member whose house was the subject of three separate drive-by shootings; once his sister was shot. One CROP member's crime partner was killed by a rival gang, who then mailed his dismembered penis to the boy's parents. Another CROP member's parents put up $60,000 to pay for his attorneys. The man was convicted of murder and sentenced to life in prison. His parents lost their home, their life savings, and had to file for bankruptcy. If you love anybody in your family, do the right thing and stop gang banging *right now!*

Diego's desire to join a gang began when he was a "bullying" victim. According to a survey released by the Josephson Institute of Ethics "50% of 43,321 respondents ages 15 to 18 said they had bullied, teased or taunted someone at least once." Violence has become a way of life in America's schools. Former Miami Dolphins and Philadelphia Eagles running back Ronnie Brown has embarked on a public speaking tour of high schools where he talks about violence and bullying. Here are Brown's *23 Ways To Stop Youth Violence*:

1. Walk away
2. See the big picture
3. Give respect to get respect
4. Think before you act
5. Learn to manage your anger
6. Talk to someone you trust
7. Listen & Understand
8. What would your family say?
9. Tell the truth
10. Speak up
11. Exhibit tolerance
12. Speak with a professional
13. Lead, don't follow
14. Adjust your attitude
15. Remember your faith
16. Think about your future
17. Know the consequences
18. Get involved at school, in your community
19. Who are you really hurting?

20. Stay in school
21. Surround yourself with positive people
22. Believe in yourself
23. Negotiate

HOW TO GET OUT OF A GANG

This chapter concludes with some tips from CROP gang members for kids who are afraid they will be killed if they want to get out of their gang.

First, you must really be willing to break the ties with the gang. If you are not strong enough to make a firm stand, you will fail and continue to be a slave they control.

Second, you must stop hanging out with gang members after school and on weekends, particularly at house parties. You do not need to notify them; just do it.

Third, you need to occupy your free time with something constructive or educational. For instance, get involved with an after school activity or sport that you like or have an interest in. You could also get a part-time job after school or help out more around the house. That way when the other gang members ask you where you have been, tell them what you have been doing so it doesn't appear that you are cutting them off completely.

Lastly, be prepared to be teased and laughed at by the other gang members, which is a form of manipulation to discourage you from doing well. They want you to do what they want to do, not what you want.

The gang members may use threats, ridicule and insults in order to persuade you to reunite with them. Their words may hurt and embarrass you, but it is only temporary. They will eventually stop harassing you when they see that you are standing firm and not allowing yourself to be provoked or drawn back in. They certainly will not kill you, which is a common myth. It is better to endure ridicule for a short period of time than to endure the suffering of living in prison, which is every gang member's eventual destination.

CHAPTER 8
The Deadly Love Triangle

Jim Bottomley's most vivid memory was of the harsh sunlight flickering off of Lake Cuyamaca. He could have attempted to run or swim to safety. Yet, he wasn't thinking about that type of escape. His plan was to commit suicide.

A 357 Magnum lay on the picnic table before Jim. A helicopter was hovering in the sky only 100 feet above. Moments earlier, Jim had watched a convoy of police vehicles enter the parking lot on the far side of the lake. They drove across a dam and onto an island where they disappeared behind a knoll. Jim had a commanding view of the lake and the island from his vantage point atop a hill. However, he had not selected the location for its magnificent view. He had chosen it for sentimental reasons. He reminisced about two idyllic afternoons he had spent there with his fiancée Maria, when they had picnicked, made love, and chatted about their impending nuptials. Forty minutes before, in the time of his greatest anguish, melancholy had seemingly drawn Jim's car to the place where he had once been deliriously happy. Maria was dead and Jim was responsible. Memories were all that he had left. He wanted to end his life too, and he had subconsciously selected a place where he could wallow in self-pity before doing the unthinkable deed.

A SWAT team spread out and crept up the brushy terrain of the knoll. Jim had an opening and could have made a break for it. But something invisible held him captive as he paced around the picnic table like a caged tiger. Jim held a cell phone in his hand. On the drive to the lake he had called his estranged wife Sarah, to say goodbye and reveal to her the location of the $16,000 secret store of cash he had hidden in his apartment. He wanted her to retrieve the money before the cops ransacked the place and stole it. Sarah had kept Jim on the phone long enough to patch in Dr. Barnes, their family psychologist. Unbeknownst to Jim, Dr.

Barnes' secretary had alerted the police department, which is how they located him. Jim was also unaware of a fact that the police negotiator was eavesdropping on the phone conversation as he spoke with Dr. Barnes.

Dr. Barnes attempted to talk Jim out of committing suicide. "Please don't do this. You are such a good man. You have played a vital role in the community for the past 25 years. You have helped so many people. No matter what the circumstances are, that is not going to change. You can still make a difference in people's lives."

Jim's gun was loaded with six bullets. He stopped pacing, sat on the bench, and gripped the gun. The cold, hard steel was somehow comforting. It was the means to Jim's desperate need to escape his own internal hell. No amount of begging by Sarah or Dr. Barnes was going to change his intention to end the personal nightmare that was his life.

"Think about your children. They will be devastated if you commit suicide. Don't you love your children?" Dr. Barnes pleaded.

"Of course I do. But I have brought shame to my family. They will be better off without me."

"We don't even know if a crime has been committed," Dr. Barnes said, pursuing a new course of action. "In your fragile mental state you may have deluded yourself into believing that Maria is dead. She may be perfectly fine. She's probably waiting for you to return to her as we speak."

Suddenly Jim was confused. The world seemed to be spinning out of control all around him. The deafening helicopter's blades were whirling over his head. The SWAT team snipers were taking up positions under the crest of the knoll. The sheer intensity of the moment was overwhelming.

"Give it up," said the police negotiator over the phone, snapping Jim out of the momentary brain freeze. "Leave the gun in the middle of the table and refrain from touching it or the police will treat your handling of the gun as a hostile act and take action accordingly."

No, Jim thought. His mind raced. If he had indeed been responsible for Maria's death, as he feared, turning himself in would result in a lifetime of misery. He needed to end it now. He gazed at the lake. It seemed so placid. There wasn't a sound. Even the cajoling voices from the phone had become silent. Jim's thoughts turned to his children, whom he loved immensely. Then Maria's radiant face flashed across his mind.

"Place the gun on the table," the police negotiator's voice barked from the phone. "Start walking toward the service road."

Throughout his 51 years, Jim had always been a man who followed the rules and respected the law. Instinctually, and somewhat mindlessly, he obeyed the officer's command. He placed the gun on the table and walked slowly toward the service road, letting out a loud shout, "No!"

"Get down on the ground," yelled one of the 10 SWAT team members who rushed Jim and tackled him to the ground.

They pinned him and handcuffed his arms behind his back. He was trapped. He was being arrested for the murder of Maria Costello, the woman he loved. In that unthinkable moment, Jim's life was vaporized.

Jim Bottomley was born and raised in the upper middle class community of La Jolla, California. He was blessed with loving parents who instilled a sense of ethics, values, and morality. As a kid, Jim was a good student who always achieved high scholastic grades. He graduated from Stanford University. He chose the legal profession and went on to law school in San Francisco. Prior to graduation, Jim met Sarah, a flight attendant, and soon they married.

After passing the bar examination, Jim started practicing law with a firm in San Jose, California. Within a year, the siren call of Southern California beckoned him home. Jim and Sarah moved south during the summer of 1976, and he landed an associate position in a small law firm in Oceanside. They were happy together, and their joyful union brought forth a son. Four years later, Jim started his own real estate and business law firm, and Sarah gave birth to twin girls. They were the perfect family of five. Jim's law firm was a success from the outset, and in 1990 he moved his practice into new, fancier digs in Carlsbad. As the business grew, Sarah and Jim bought a series of increasingly larger homes and invested in a growing retirement account. They took numerous local trips and travelled often to Mexico, Hawaii, Mammoth Mountain, Lake Tahoe, San Francisco, and even Tahiti and the Caribbean. To outside observers, they were a typical baby boomer family. They had monetary success, a close, active family, and a seemingly bright future ahead.

Jim's world seemed perfect, yet inner happiness eluded him. His daily life felt like a roller coaster of emotions. Periodic depression seemed to be an integral part of his existence. In 1985, only four years after the birth of his twins and the founding of his law firm, Jim consulted with the psychologist Dr. Barnes. In 1985 psychologists rarely favored Prozac or other anti-depressant medication. The only viable treatment was talk therapy. Following some initial conversations, Dr. Barnes concluded that Jim's depression resulted from hyper-responsibility syndrome; he was addicted to taking care of his family and clients. He was constantly worrying about their happiness and success. As a result, he took on much more responsibility than he could handle, including things that Sarah, who was no longer employed, should have done, such as shopping and dry cleaning. Jim was obsessed with coaching all of his kids' sports teams, which he did for more than 10 years. It was very time-consuming. Jim was also hyper-responsible with his clients, which led to extra time spent at work. There were simply not enough hours in the day. The result was that Jim never got enough sleep and rarely had any recreation time. He was always in a hurry and under stress. When Jim became overwhelmed by his many responsibilities, his mood would plummet. Dr. Barnes determined that Jim suffered from chronic depression, which was a common diagnosis for someone afflicted with what is known today as bipolar disorder.

Dr. Barnes ultimately discovered that low self-esteem was the root cause of Jim's insatiable need to be hyper-responsible with everyone in his life. When Jim was a kid, he had an older brother who picked on him and parents who demanded that he be near perfect in schoolwork and sports. He was overweight and not as athletic as his older brother. Jim felt that his parents favored his brother, who was an exceptional student and gifted athlete. Kids at school ridiculed him because of his weight. During adolescence he felt fat, ugly, and undesirable. He felt shy and inadequate around girls. His only date in high school cancelled at the last minute. His college girlfriend, who he felt was the love of his life, dumped him for another man, and his law school girlfriend dumped him for a wealthy guy. These incidents deepened his underlying low self-esteem.

Jim's feelings of inadequacy pervaded his relationship with his wife. Throughout their marriage Jim feared that Sarah was unhappy because of his perceived shortcomings as a husband. He was constantly striving to discover what would make her happy. Sarah blamed Jim for many of the actual and perceived problems in her life. In his mind, he was never good enough for her.

Jim and Sarah had their 25th wedding anniversary during the winter of 1999. By then Jim had become increasingly disenchanted with their relationship, and he was certain that she was, too. The things that made him happy — surfing, golf with his buddies, hiking, going to the beach — were things in which she had lost interest. Sarah didn't want to do anything with Jim anymore — go to the movies or out to nightclubs. Jim felt that nothing seemed to excite her. Jim feared they were no longer compatible. In another year the twins would be going off to college and Jim would be alone in the house with Sarah. He worried that they would have nothing to talk about because they no longer had much in common. Jim was also bothered by the fact that Sarah refused to seek work, despite the fact that money was tight.

For her part, Sarah was easily annoyed by Jim's quirkiness and various other symptoms of what she (as a psychology student and amateur psychologist) referred to as "manic depression." Sarah thought Jim was moody and volatile. He became angry easily and refused to accept criticism. He was so up and down. On vacations he was vibrant, animated, and excitable. He wanted to make love constantly. However, at home he was a pack-rat and saved everything he had ever acquired. His garage was overflowing to the rafters. She also didn't understand why a 50-year-old man had become obsessed with surfing and spending so much time on his own.

During a vacation in Mazatlan, Jim met a middle-aged, heavy-set man on the beach who turned out to be an excellent surfer. As a kid, surfing had been one of Jim's passions. Jim borrowed the man's surfboard and had a blast. He felt young again. When they returned to San Diego, Jim surfed at every opportunity. He even took his surfboard to his office.

Jim surfed every day after work until past sunset, every weekend day, and often even on vacation. As Jim rekindled his love affair with surfing, he and Sarah were drifting further and further apart. Jim's passion for riding waves served to be a substitute for the passion that no longer existed in their marriage.

Although otherwise dissatisfied with his marriage, Jim had never cheated on Sarah. However, that fidelity changed early in the summer of 1999 on a guys' golf trip to Mexico. Jim accompanied his friends to a bar. Jim got drunk, met a young woman, named Lulu, and one thing led to another.

Three weeks prior to cheating on Sarah with Lulu, Jim met Maria. She had retained Jim to do legal work concerning a bitter dispute with her ex-husband involving their former home. He was contending that Maria owed him more than $50,000; whereas she was claiming that she previously paid him that amount in cash. He also disputed her sole ownership of the large house in which they had previously lived together. He contended that their Marital Settlement Agreement was invalid. Maria disputed this, and wanted to retain the house for herself. It had increased considerably in value, and she didn't want to share the sale proceeds with him. A domestic attorney was handling the divorce aspects of the dispute, and Maria hired Jim to represent her on the real estate issues. Jim was able to solve her legal issues, and Maria seemed quite pleased with his diligent and skilled assistance.

Maria was a 45-year-old Filipino immigrant who worked as a registered nurse. From the first day she walked into Jim's law office, he was attracted to her exotic beauty. He thought about her constantly and wondered if she would be interested in him romantically. Jim decided to explore the possibility.

"I find you to be one of the most beautiful women I've ever laid eyes on. Would you be interested in dating me?"

"Well, you're married," Maria responded, pointing to Jim's

wedding band.

"I'm going to do something about that," Jim blurted out, articulating for the first time a consideration that had been weighing on him for months.

"Call me when you do," Maria replied, leaving no doubt in Jim's mind that the physical attraction was mutual.

Jim had always taken great pride in his personal code of ethics. The indiscretion with Lulu had caused him to feel a sense of shame and guilt he had never before known. And now he was asking a woman out on a date! He did not want to be a man who cheated on his wife. Sarah had been a kind and caring wife. Although Jim no longer loved Sarah romantically, he respected her and knew that he had to own up to his failures as a husband. He told Sarah about the infidelity. She was terribly upset and kicked Jim out of the house. He never spent another night at home with his wife.

Two weeks later Jim asked Maria out on a date, and she consented. Jim was in seventh Heaven. Maria told Jim she had not dated anyone since her separation because she was so turned off from men due to being traumatized during the relationship. It was a bold-faced lie, the first of many she would spin in a web of deceit that would capture Jim's heart and later rip it to shreds. Jim was unaware that Maria was a woman who harbored many deep, dark secrets. His gradual discovery of her sordid truth pierced the threshold of his sanity. As the true Maria revealed herself, it propelled Jim on a torturous journey from which he would never recover.

The whirlwind romance of Jim and Maria began with a dinner date that concluded with passion — incandescent passion. Maria possessed a sexual appetite that was bold, exciting, and seemingly insatiable. Over the next month they were together almost every night. Jim took Maria to Lake Tahoe for a romantic weekend getaway, and she told him she loved him. Two weeks later the couple went to Catalina Island to attend a jazz festival, and Jim told her that he loved her, too. Jim was so swept away by Maria that he asked her to marry him after only six weeks of dating. When Maria replied, "I would love to," Jim felt a rush of euphoria that he hoped would last forever.

Maria reignited Jim's zest for life and fulfilled an inner longing to be appreciated by someone special. Maria was complimentary and interested in Jim. She said more nice things about him than anyone he had ever met. She also seemed vulnerable, which played right into Jim's desire to help her win her legal battle with her ex-husband and recapture her happiness. Their relationship seemed to be the salvation of Jim's discontent as well as Maria's.

Jim kept a journal, which he wrote in daily. In one telling entry he wrote: "I love Maria, and she loves me so much. She makes me feel better, whether I'm with her or just talking on the phone, than anyone ever has in my life. I feel like she has lifted me up to heaven. She's my guardian angel; my good luck charm."

Jim and Maria were inseparable during the first few months of their relationship. Most evenings she would cook him dinner and Jim would assist her. They frequently ate outdoors on her patio. They had wonderful, loving times together at the Street Scene Music Festival, clubs, Cuyamaca Lake, Seaport Village, golfing at the range, Disneyland, and shopping. They frequently went to the mountains or the beach where they played and teased each other like high school kids. Their relationship was a source of great joy for Jim. They planned to marry as soon as Jim's divorce was finalized. They seemed thrilled to be in one another's arms.

However, three months into their seemingly beautiful relationship, Maria began to act erratically. She cancelled dates at the last minute with what appeared to be highly concocted excuses, and sometimes without even calling Jim. She refused to allow Jim to have any contact with her family members. Jim did not know that Maria was cheating on him with at least two other men. These men included Tom, a handsome young tradesman, and Kelly, a wealthy, retired industrialist.

In the beginning of their relationship Jim had no reason to distrust Maria and never considered the possibility that she was having relations with another man. She frequently called him late at night to express her love and devotion. Jim assumed that she was calling from bed, thinking of him prior to falling asleep. He was madly in love, and she seemed to share his feelings.

Gradually, however, suspicion began to creep into Jim's

thoughts. When a beautiful bouquet of flowers appeared at Maria's home, he asked her about its origin. Maria assured Jim they were from a female patient she had treated at the dialysis clinic where she worked. On another occasion Maria insisted that she tell Jim's family that she was merely a guest at a dinner party Jim gave for relatives, and she refused to allow him to characterize her as his fiancée or even his girlfriend. Even more disconcerting was an evening when Tom showed up at her house unannounced and attempted to hug her in Jim's presence. When Jim questioned Maria about Tom, she admitted that he had asked her out but that she wasn't interested. It was a lie.

These and other incidents raised Jim's suspicions and created a great amount of stress and anxiety. Yet, he could not allow himself to get angry at Maria. She made it clear on several occasions that something she hated about her former husband was his terrible temper and that he was constantly displaying his anger at her. In order to avoid her resentment, Jim internalized his feelings whenever he got mad at her. Over time those toxic emotions built up and caused Jim's anxiety to blind his sense of reason.

Maria constantly left her options open until the very last minute. She would rarely commit to taking any course of action, which increased Jim's frustration as the months passed. There were times when she would not be at home early in the morning and would not answer her cell phone. This behavior caused Jim to experience paranoia that she was sleeping at another man's house.

More suspicions arose one evening when Maria made Jim dinner at her home. Someone called her home phone, and Maria went into another room so that Jim could not hear the conversation. Shortly thereafter, a man (who Jim later learned was Kelly) was knocking on the front door. Maria panicked and asked Jim to hide upstairs while she got rid of him. When Jim protested, Maria concocted a ridiculous story. Jim went along with the rouse and listened while Maria told Kelly that she could not go out with him that night. At that point Jim knew something was wrong, but he was so lovesick that he ignored the obvious and chose not to confront her.

Maria asked Jim to review the legal files related to her

divorce case, which he did. In doing so, Jim came across a letter and a psychological report on Maria's ex-husband in which many allegations were made by him and his attorney that Maria had cheated with, among others, Kelly. There were many other insidious remarks about the woman Jim planned to marry contained in those records, and he wondered why she would allow him to read the information. Jim questioned Maria about the purported indiscretions.

"It's all lies and slander from a spurned husband," Maria had responded. "Kelly is just a friend. He's 75 years old. Do you honestly think I would have sex with an old man? Yuk!"

Jim believed her because his love for Maria had blinded him to the obvious. However, now that he had been alerted to the possibility of infidelity, he began to question her suspicious behavior. Maria seemed to be bonded to her cell phone. She would often receive calls in Jim's presence and speak in hushed tones or scurry off to another room. People would call her house at 5:00 a.m. and wake them up when they were sleeping together. One time Jim knew that she was speaking to Tom and threatened to cancel a romantic getaway to Las Vegas they had planned. Maria told the caller never to bother her again, but Jim suspected that he had already hung up the phone. On another occasion Jim questioned whether a 5:00 a.m. call was really from a co-worker named Angie. Maria got angry and chastised him for not trusting her.

On another evening when they were together at her house, Maria showed Jim a packet of photos, which were mainly of the two of them. However, there were about eight photos of Maria in sexy poses on her exer-cycle with the same flower bouquet that she claimed was a gift sent by one of her patients.

"Who took these photos?" Jim asked.

"You did, silly. Don't you remember?" Maria lied.

"No, I didn't," Jim responded as he studied the photos more carefully. "Look, these photos are stamp-dated October 25. I was attending a convention in Las Vegas on that day."

"You must be mistaken."

"Would you like to see the hotel records?" Jim responded sarcastically, angry that he had caught her in an outright lie.

He drove home simmering with anger that night. His mind was racing. What other lies were there? Were her ex-husband's allegations about an affair with Kelly true? And what about Tom, the man who tried to hug Maria affectionately in Jim's presence? All of Jim's suspicions were bubbling to the surface.

Despite professing her love for Jim, Maria continued to be deceitful. When Jim discovered that Tom was still sniffing around, he pressed Maria for details, and she inferred that Tom was stalking her. Jim drafted a Cease and Desist letter from Maria to Tom demanding that he stay away from her and refrains from calling her. Maria signed the letter, which further stated that Maria and Jim were getting married. However, as they came close to his shop to deliver the letter, Maria reneged, pitched a fit, and refused to let Jim get out of the car.

Later Jim confronted Tom. "Can I speak to you for a moment concerning Maria Costello?"

"What would you like to know?" the younger man asked.

"Maria told me that you have been stalking her."

"What? That's ridiculous."

"What is the exact nature of your relationship with Maria?" Jim pressed.

"Who wants to know?"

"Her angry fiancé." Jim's tone left no doubt regarding the seriousness of his inquiry.

"Dude, there is no relationship. We hooked up last year. Then we went out on a couple of dates, but that was it. She keeps calling me and asking when we can get together again, but I really wasn't that into her. Now that I know she has a fiancé, I'm out."

When Jim confronted Maria about his conversation with Tom, she denounced Tom as a liar. He did not believe her. Maria's dishonesty forced Jim to consider breaking up with her.

That evening Jim made a list of all the things that he loved about Maria:

(1) She is exotic and beautiful.

(2) She is intelligent.

(3) She is witty and clever.

(4) She is so much fun to be with and to do things with.

(5) She seems genuinely interested in me and the things I

like.

(6) She loves children.

(7) She has a warm, tender smile.

(8) She is very complimentary.

(9) She is a great conversationalist.

(10) She has a sexy accent.

(11) She is a terrific lover.

(12) She loves to take showers together.

(13) There are times when she is sweet and loving.

As Jim studied the list, he remembered all of the reasons why he had proposed to Maria in the first place. He was going to overlook her flaws because he was madly in love. He was putty in her hands and easily manipulated into turning the other cheek. When he should have laid down the law and become angry and assertive with her, he had great difficulty doing so. Deep down he was afraid of losing her.

Maria began to take Jim for granted. At the last minute, she cancelled several dates they had planned. He also caught Maria lying on numerous occasions. Jim finally got fed up and confronted Maria about her deceitfulness. The confrontation resulted in a huge fight.

After confronting Maria, Jim wrote in his journal: *One day I'm on a cloud with our plans for a future together, and then the next it's, "I'm not comfortable with our relationship," and we almost break up. It's a struggle — I'm fighting every day to persevere in our relationship and our future together and my sanity. Is it worth it? Or should I just let it go? What would I have? The loneliness of a single's life in a cold apartment; the beautiful, haunting memories of a life with Maria that was, and could have been, but for our fatal flaws.*

Over the next month circumstantial evidence that Maria was having an affair with Kelly began to mount. Jim caught Maria red-handed spending the night at Kelly's. Maria claimed that the overnight visit was in a nurse/ health care provider role and that she had obligations "to care for him." She reiterated that the relationship was not sexual and that she did not sleep in his bed. On a separate occasion she lied when she said that she was going to visit her minister, but it really turned out to be Kelly. Yet another time she left Jim's apartment at 1:00 in the morning, supposedly heading home for the night, but instead went to Kelly's condo.

Still, after all of the obvious signs of deceit, Jim remained blinded by his love for Maria and entranced by her sexual magnitude. He was so enchanted by Maria that he rationalized her many lies and much of her bad behavior. Jim was fooling himself; living in a dangerous fantasy world.

Marie was a master at keeping Jim mesmerized, infatuated, and off balance. If there was a college course in the art of seducing and manipulating men, Maria would have been professor emeritus. On many occasions she would plan erotic surprises that took Jim's breath away. At other times she would express her unbridled love, and Jim felt as though he was the happiest person on the planet. He was manically enthralled one day and severely depressed the next.

Maria continued to plan, promise, and then cancel engagements as Jim toiled on the legal work for her upcoming trial in the dispute with her husband. She invited Jim to go to the big boat show in San Diego, but canceled at the last minute. She also canceled their date to attend a jazz concert that same night. In a telephone conversation just a couple of days later Maria told Jim, "All day long I have been thinking of you with a lot of love." He noted in his journal that she sounded genuine. Yet, that night they had a date, and when Jim went to meet her at work, she said that she had to meet Kelly briefly, and she left Jim at her house to await her return. Jim waited all night, and Maria did not return until 4:45 in the morning.

The pressures of the relationship began to adversely affect Jim's mental health. His stress over the Kelly situation began to manifest itself in all aspects of his life. He experienced wild mood swings, a loss of concentration and focus at work, diminishing contact with friends, a lack of interest with surfing or golf or working out, crying, pounding-the-floor tantrums, staying in bed with his head under the covers, scratching his skin until sores appeared and then picking at them, and throwing his cell phone. He was simply going berserk.

Jim and Maria had a big argument over the nature of her relationship with Kelly, and during the heat of it Jim forced her to the ground with the palm of his hand. It sprained Maria's knee. Never in his life had Jim hit or hurt a woman. He despised violence. He recognized that he was suffering from a mental breakdown and the next day he again sought professional help.

Jim initially contacted Dr. Barnes, who had seen him periodically for depression and anxiety over the preceding 14 years. Dr. Barnes could not treat Jim because he was once again treating Sarah, which would have been a conflict of interest. He recommended one of his colleagues, Dr. Elle Stanton. Over the next two months Jim had many long sessions with Dr. Stanton, which focused primarily on the emotional roller coaster that was his relationship with Maria. In describing the Kelly situation, Jim projected himself as Maria's savior. He wanted to help her pull away from what he perceived as an immoral attraction to Kelly's money and the things it could buy. Jim experienced great sadness over the thought of losing Maria. She was his true love — the person he wished to live out the rest of his days with, and who he thought felt the same way about him. For some crazy reason, he couldn't live without her. He feared the single life, feared being alone, and didn't want to lose his second chance at happiness.

While most of their conversations focused on Maria, Jim also expressed sadness about being separated from Sarah and his children. Sarah had spoken to Jim about a possible reconciliation and suggested they begin marriage counseling immediately. Dr. Stanton surmised that Jim was focusing too much of his mental energy on Maria and saw his relationship with her as his primary purpose in life. He was clearly torn between distrust and disapproval, sympathy for what he thought she was going through, and the belief that he could save her. In that his marriage was already fraying before he met Maria, his relationship with her seemed to be both a symptom of, and a trigger for, his declining mental health. Dr. Stanton advised Jim to explore marital counseling with Sarah and recommended that he see her colleague, Dr. Frank Nelson, a psychiatrist, who could prescribe the appropriate medication for Jim.

Based on Dr. Stanton's referral, Jim met with Dr. Nelson. He casually listened to a portion of Jim's tale of woe concerning his relationship with Maria, but he made no notes, administered no tests, and merely prescribed an anti-depressant. However, the anti-depressant had other side effects that disrupted Jim's inner world, including increased anxiety, nervousness, racing thoughts, and restlessness. He was only sleeping two hours a night. He continued to take the anti-depressant because he was desperate to find a cure for his depression and anxiety.

The anti-depressant also intensified Jim's paranoia that Maria was cheating on him with Kelly. Maria had assured Jim on several occasions that Kelly never spent the night at her house. Yet, when he drove out early one morning to deliver a letter and some Starbucks coffee to her, he found a white pick-up truck in the driveway. Maria assured Jim that it was her brother's truck, which she had borrowed to use over the weekend. Jim didn't believe her. He had written down the truck's license plate number and retained the services of a private investigator to ascertain the truck owner's name. It turned out to be Kelly. At that point Jim had had enough. He decided to break up with Maria.

Jim met Maria outside her place of employment following her work shift. He informed her that he was breaking off the engagement because of her lies concerning Kelly. Maria pleaded with Jim not to end their relationship, but he held strong to his conviction that it was over. He also insisted to be paid the $2,400 that she owed him for legal services from the previous summer. Maria became angry at the thought of paying Jim, but she reluctantly wrote him a check.

The next morning, after cashing the check, Jim went to Maria's house to collect his belongings. Maria professed her love and begged Jim not to break off their engagement. She reiterated that her relationship with Kelly was platonic and promised to stop seeing him. Jim's physical attraction to Maria was practically irresistible. He was also a fiercely competitive man. The thought of losing Maria to a wealthy old man infuriated him. Driven by his desire to beat Kelly and his lust for Maria, Jim made the fatal decision to take her back.

In the mean time, Jim and Sarah had attended one marital counseling session that focused primarily on the rules of engagement for moving forward. When Jim cancelled the next session, Sarah smelled a rat and asked Jim if he was seeing another woman. Jim admitted that he was. Sarah went ballistic and told him to, "Go to hell." That night Sarah attempted suicide by taking an overdose of valium and alcohol. Fortunately, she was not successful. Jim was emotionally devastated when he learned that his actions had hurt Sarah so deeply. He broke down and cried, because he still cared for Sarah and because he knew the possibility of their reconciliation was lost forever.

Jim's final unraveling began when he had dinner with Maria's sister, Rosa, and her husband to go over her testimony at Maria's upcoming domestic trial. Rosa was scheduled to be the star witness. However, Jim discovered some discrepancies between Rosa's and Maria's version of events of key facts in the case, which led Jim to believe that Maria was lying about giving her husband the $50,000 in cash. Jim took this opportunity to inquire about Rosa's understanding of Maria's relationship with Kelly. Her response broke his heart and changed the course of his life forever.

Rosa said, "Maria has always deceived, manipulated, and taken advantage of men. She and Kelly started having an affair at least a year before they left their respective spouses. Then they lived together in a motel until they moved into Kelly's condo. Kelly went on a trip with my family; he and Maria slept together. Everyone knows that Maria is only after Kelly for his money. She's kind of like his sex slave. You know Maria's perky breasts? They are not real. She had breast enlargement surgery and Kelly paid for it."

Jim was floored by the sordid revelations. He became violently sick to his stomach, excused himself to the restroom, and threw up in the toilet. He tried to revive himself by splashing cold water on his face. When Jim returned to the table, Rosa delivered the coup de grâce: "There is more to the story. Maria wants to marry Kelly so she can get her greedy hands on his money, but Kelly refused. So Maria left him and returned to her own place. Then you came into the picture. Maria told me, 'I'm dating this handsome, successful lawyer. I'm going to use him to make Kelly jealous.' And it worked. Kelly proposed marriage recently, and Maria said yes. She is a manipulative, cunning little bitch." Rosa went on to describe a long line of men who Maria had swindled. It was shocking.

Jim left the restaurant in a daze. He drove directly to Maria's house to confront her, but she was not there. He went home and tried to call Maria on her cell phone, but there was no answer. Jim got drunk and replayed his conversation with Rosa over and over again. He thought about the many times Maria had spent the night at Kelly's and what a fool he had been. He became sick again when he realized there must have been times when Maria left Kelly's bed and then jumped into his own. He considered the future implications of his law career if Maria really did have an extra-marital affair with Kelly, meaning her husband's lawsuit against her would be a valid one. Even worse, he realized that Maria was using him to perpetrate a fraud. Maria's ex-husband's lawyer had recently reminded Jim that Maria assumed a $35,000 bank loan as part of the Marital Settlement Agreement. Maria had used a friend of hers to negotiate a $7,000 settlement with the bank that freed her from further obligation. However, the bank sued Maria's ex-husband for the $28,000 balance plus interest and Jim now realized that Maria was on the hook for that amount. Jim further surmised that Maria had lied about giving the $50,000 in cash to her ex-husband and she had instead used the money to purchase a Mercedes. He thought about her intense anger when Jim demanded payment for his legal services, and he sensed that she had never intended to pay him. Was their entire romance a manipulation based on Maria's ulterior motive of winning the domestic lawsuit against her ex-husband by using a trusting lawyer? Was Jim a pawn in Maria's chess match to gain Kelly's hand in marriage? If it was all true — the deceit, lies, greed, betrayal, secret life — then it meant that Maria had made a mockery of Jim's love for her. This unfathomable insight forced Jim to further realize that his infatuation with Maria had played a major part of his decision to leave Sarah and cause his wife to experience unspeakable misery. How could he have been such a dimwit?

Throughout the night Jim tried to sleep but he couldn't. His mind raced over and over about the questions surrounding Maria. He thought back to the amazing times he had with her, their extraordinary sex life and her countless professions of love. No one could fake that...or could they? On the one hand, he knew that she had been deceitful; on the other, he was certain their love was real. He even considered the possibility the Maria and Rosa were involved in some kind of sibling rivalry and that Rosa had deliberately lied to him in order to lash out at her sister.

Jim had a romantic date planned with Maria for the next morning. He again replayed his conversation with Rosa in his head, and he imagined himself laying out the litany of lies and deceit before Maria like a prosecutor cross-examining a witness. He also planned to use the date to reach a final resolution concerning the Kelly situation. Jim was going to issue an ultimatum to Maria: choose him or me. Despite everything that Rosa had said, Jim was still hopelessly in love with Maria. He knew in his heart that she felt the same way. He wanted to give her one final opportunity to prove that love by ending the relationship with Kelly.

Maria was due at Jim's apartment by 8:30 a.m. for their scheduled date. As usual, she was late. After waiting anxiously for an hour Jim, called and reached Maria at her home.

"Hello," Maria answered the phone.

"It's Jim. What are you doing? We had a date this morning. Remember?"

"I don't think that I should come to your apartment." Maria sounded shaky and fearful. She dropped her voice very low. "Kelly hired two private investigators to keep surveillance on both of us. One of them is probably watching your apartment right now."

"What?" Jim was unnerved by the information. Maria had told Jim that Kelly carried two loaded pistols with him at all times. Jim had purchased a gun because he was afraid for his life, and for Maria's. "We have to talk, right now, Maria. I've had it with this Kelly situation."

Maria agreed to meet Jim at a neutral location — the parking lot at Nordstrom's in Escondido. Jim was physically and emotionally exhausted. He was also hung over from all his drinking the night before, and was not thinking clearly. His plan was to confront Maria about the things Rosa had said, and to tell her to choose between him and Kelly once and for all. Yet, somewhere in the back of his mind, Jim harbored thoughts of a romantic date that he and Maria had previously planned. The degree of his confused intentions was evidenced by the fact that he searched for his vile of Viagra pills before departing. He found them in his backpack, which was where Jim kept the gun. He took a pill and considered the gun. In that moment he remembered that Kelly had twice used the threat of suicide to gain Maria's affection. He decided that he may use a similar ploy to force Maria to finally sever ties with Kelly, so he took the backpack with him.

Jim arrived ten minutes late at the Nordstrom's parking lot and looked around for Maria's car. He waited and waited. She didn't show. Jim called Maria from his cell phone. She answered, and as soon as she heard Jim's voice she began speaking in her native Tagalog, which she often spoke with her relatives. Jim surmised that Kelly was in the house. He wasn't about to spend another day obsessing about Maria and Kelly being together. He became angry and confrontational.

"I'm coming over right now," Jim said. "I need answers. If Kelly is there, then the three of us can talk this out together."

As Jim hung up the phone he realized that the three of them talking together was exactly what Dr. Nelson had suggested to resolve the conflict. Jim could not shake his anger. It drove him as he drove the car. He needed answers. If Maria really was in love with Kelly and she chose him, Jim would be crushed, but he would walk away. He felt a small sense of relief that soon it would all be over.

Jim turned the corner onto Maria's street and saw Kelly's pick-up truck parked out of view of anyone driving past Maria's house. Why did he hide his truck? The question forced another more serious question to surface: What about the two loaded pistols Kelly supposedly kept with him at all times? The voice of reason screamed in Jim's head, *why am I doing this?* The voice of an obsessed lover shouted back, *because I need to know. I cannot leave without knowing the truth. I want Maria for the rest of my life. What does she want?*

Jim's head was pounding. He started to sweat. His body was tense. His anxiety was at a boiling point. Jim parked his car in Maria's driveway. He threw the backpack over one shoulder and headed for the front door. He knocked on the door and then rang twice.

The door finally opened and Maria came into view. She nervously said, "Hi, come on in."

As Jim entered the house, his thoughts turned to Kelly. Where was he? Should Jim be concerned? "Where is Kelly?" he asked.

She replied, "I don't know."

"I saw his truck parked up and around the corner," Jim retorted, as he gestured to the area like it was a toxic waste dump. "I know he is here, Maria. Don't lie to me."

After a long pause Maria finally answered, "No Jim, he's not here. He is not in the house." Maria seemed to diminish a few sizes during the exchange, as if she was trying to get small enough to disappear through a crack in the tile floor.

"You are lying. Do you really think that I am that stupid? Kelly is here, either inside the house or snooping around up there." Jim pointed to the hillside beyond the front yard.

Maria changed the subject, "What did Rosa and Mario tell you?"

"She contradicted you. They both did. Regarding the meeting with your ex-husband, she said that the three of you left him at the house with the cash in the safe." Maria began to shake her head vigorously as Jim continued. "You said that the three of you remained here in the family room, and that he left carrying all the cash in a brown envelope."

"What does it matter?"

"Isn't that obvious? Your version suggests that you paid the $50,000 in cash and that he left with the money in his possession. But your sister's version suggests that the cash remained here in the safe. This supports his position that you stole the cash while you still had access to the safe. You did steal it from him, didn't you? You stole it and bought your car with it."

Maria didn't respond.

"You ripped off your husband." The revelation was hitting Jim as he said the words. It all suddenly made sense: "Huh? Maria? And you've been lying about it ever since, haven't you? You lied to *me* about it... not only me as your fiancé, but me as your attorney! You planned to lie about it on the stand... under oath! And you saw nothing wrong with using me to put on your perjured testimony! I was part of your plan. It would be easy to get me to cooperate... I wouldn't even have to know the truth... better if I didn't. You knew that I would believe you, and stand by you — and most importantly, trust you. You knew it all would work when you knew I had fallen in love with you. In the end, as long as you beat him, you didn't care about my reputation or my legal license. And you especially didn't care about me."

After a long pause, Maria asked, "What else did Rosa tell you?"

"She said that you and Kelly were having an affair together even before you both separated from your spouses. She said that was one of the main reasons that your husband acted so badly with you. He caught you... something to do with credit card receipts. She said that you and Kelly spent nights together in hotels, and you even slept for two or three nights in the same room on a family trip to Santa Maria. How could you lie to me about that all along, Maria? You assured me that you had never slept with Kelly or had sex with him. Everything you told me about your relationship was a lie."

"No, no," she said, as if listening to something outside. Then suddenly she said, "I can't talk about it right now."

Jim stammered on. "Your sister also told me you were previously married while you were in the Philippines, to a guy named Bernie, and you took advantage of 'poor ol' Bernie' for jewels and clothes and make-up and cash — all the things you still crave. And she told me that you had lots of boyfriends in Chicago... and that you used and manipulated every one of them for jewels and cash. She said that you got your townhouse by scamming an insurance company or something. She said that your whole life has been about manipulating, using, and lying to men."

"That bitch!" Maria exclaimed.

"She also told me that you would try to deny that you and Kelly had an affair, but that your husband has proof that you stayed in hotels and ate at restaurants with him. She said he plans to bring all this out at the hearing. Why, Maria? Why did you lie to me about everything? I love you so much. I don't understand why you did this to me."

Maria responded in a cold voice, "Just cancel it."

"Cancel what?"

"The hearing next week. I won't go. Give him everything. I don't want anything," Maria said, essentially admitting that what Rosa said about her ripping off her ex-husband was all true.

Jim exploded. "You lied to me about everything. You are a pathological liar. You used me for your greedy purpose…to rip off your ex-husband…to snare Kelly…to satisfy your lust for material things." Jim added cynically, "There was only one problem with your little scheme, Maria. You fell in love with me. That's what you always told me… and I was so happy. By some miracle you fell in love with me at the start and you never lost that love."

For a fleeting second as he spoke of their love, Jim felt forgiveness. He was jerked back to reality when Maria said, "Oh, yeah!" The words came out of her mouth in a disdainful, cynical tone. Her stare was cold as ice. Jim looked into her eyes and at that moment the truth was revealed. She never loved him. Jim's fragile mental state shattered into a million pieces. What happened next was the very definition of "temporary insanity."

Jim reached into his backpack, pulled out the gun, and put it to his head. Maria screamed and came toward Jim. He stared into her eyes, and for a brief moment, his hand started to tighten on the trigger. Then he turned the gun toward Maria and emptied the revolver into her face. Bam! Bam! Bam! Bam! Bam! Bam! Maria was dead before her body hit the tile floor.

Jim Bottomley was tried and convicted of second degree murder for killing Maria Costello, the woman he loved. He received a mandatory sentence of 15 years to life and an additional 25-year enhancement for using a gun.

What lessons can be learned from Jim's story? Here are five to consider: (1) Jim should have walked away from the relationship soon as bad things started to occur. (2) There is no reason ever to carry a gun because you may end up using it, causing tragedy. (3) When you are in trouble in your life, you should turn to your family and friends for guidance. (4) It is best not to try to control things that you cannot control. (5) Don't think only about yourself.

CHAPTER 9
The Mexican Gang Member

Thirty-three-year-old Johnny Alverez was a gang member known as the "Rooftop Bandit" to the Los Angeles County Police officers who were diligently searching for him. Johnny's first rooftop burglary occurred at the Azusa Jewelers located in a West Covina strip center. Johnny had noticed a large aluminum fan on the ceiling of the jewelry store. He had once seen a movie where burglars had entered a dwelling through a similar fan, and decided to try it out.

At 2:00 a.m. Johnny made his way to the rooftop with a car jack and a sledge hammer. He used the jack to pry the fan casing from its mounts. He kicked at the fan's blades until he had created a hole through which he entered the ceiling of the store. He maneuvered past gas lines and water pipes, steadied himself on a 2'x4' support beam, and busted through the sheet rock ceiling. It was only 12 feet to the ground. Johnny jumped and was inside the jewelry store.

Johnny first secured an escape route. He stacked two tables upon a partition wall so that he could climb to the roof. Then he searched for jewelry. Below one empty case he found a box in a drawer that contained numerous small envelopes filled with rings, bracelets, and necklaces that needed repair. Only one of the display cases contained any jewelry, and it was locked. Johnny used the sledge hammer to bust through the inch thick glass. It took ten wallops before the glass finally shattered. A loud alarm sounded. Johnny panicked and got out of there fast.

Johnny took the loot to San Diego, where he met Julio, a fence from Mexico. Julio was a drug smuggler and a family friend. He gave Johnny $5,000 and 10 ounces of cocaine for the stolen jewelry. It was party time. Johnny called several homeboys from his gang in Florence and told them that he had come up. Johnny and his homeboys went to Mexico, where they got a hotel room and partied for a month. When the drugs and the money finally ran out, Johnny returned to Los Angeles to commit another burglary. This was the life of a gang member — boom or bust.

Johnny wanted to burglarize another jewelry store, but the alarms were a deterrent. One day he noticed a work truck at a construction site with a door medallion that read "West Covina Alarms." He staked out the truck. When the owner returned, Johnny approached him.

"Excuse me, homie. Can I talk to you?"

"What do you want?" The man studied Johnny suspiciously.

Johnny was covered from head to toe with blue ink prison tattoos. He was obviously a hardcore Mexican gang member.

"I'm Johnny," he said, smiling broadly and extending an inviting hand.

"I'm Mark." The truck owner shook Johnny's hand.

"I just got out of prison. A month ago, I burglarized a jewelry store. I had a way to get in, but when I smashed a case open, the alarm went off. If you could take the alarms apart, I'll do all the stealing. We could make bank working together."

Mark shook his head and laughed. "I could use some extra cash. Don't trip, I've got you covered."

The two men drove around until they located a jewelry store in a strip mall that had an aluminum ceiling fan. That night, around 1:00 a.m., Mark went to the strip center with his tool box. He opened a box on the side of the building and disabled the jewelry store's alarm. He called Johnny. "It's done. Now, do your thing."

Johnny had hired one of the neighborhood drug addicts named Smiley to do the burglary with him. Johnny went through the roof as he had done before. Once he was inside the jewelry store, he filled a back pack with watches, gold chains, wedding rings, earrings, and bracelets. It was a massive haul. Johnny escaped without a hitch. Julio the fence paid him $7,000 in cash and 100 grams of heroin. Johnny gave Mark $2,500, and he paid Smiley $500 and two grams of heroin. Smiley was overjoyed. He gave Johnny a strong hug and told him, "I will do any crime with you."

With Mark's assistance, Johnny robbed a total of seven jewelry stores over a four-month period. For each job he recruited a different heroin addict to assist him. The crimes became increasingly sophisticated. Johnny fashioned a rope with knots in order to quickly climb out of the jewelry stores. When he encountered a safe in one of the stores, he recalled the same movie about the burglar. In the movie the jewel thief used a small cutting torch to access the safes. Johnny purchased a small, powerful gas torch and found that he could replicate the scene from the movie. Mark's monetary fee increased with each job until Johnny learned that Mark was addicted to methamphetamines. Johnny found a meth dealer, and traded jewelry for drugs. He kept Mark well supplied with meth, and motivated.

Johnny was living the high life. He'd do a job, sell the jewelry to the fence, and then party in Mexico. Yet, problems arose on the eighth jewelry store that he burglarized.

Johnny and his drug addict crime partner had no difficulty entering the Zale's Jewelry Store through the rooftop fan. Once he was inside, Johnny emptied jewelry from all of the display cases. Then he spotted a huge metal safe. He removed the cutting torch from his backpack and went to work. He cut a hole around the combination lock which was centered on the safe. Once the lock was removed, the safe door opened. Johnny was overjoyed to see that it was full of cash and finely-cut diamonds — more money and jewels than he had ever seen. It was the ultimate score.

What Johnny did not detect was the safe's silent alarm, which was directly connected to the West Covina Police Department. When he opened the safe, the alarm was triggered, and several squad cars were immediately dispatched to the jewelry store. Johnny knew that he was in trouble when he saw flashlights shining through the glass storefront. He hoped to escape through his rooftop hole, but discovered that there was a helicopter hovering above the building, shining a light directly on his hole. Johnny was trapped inside the jewelry store.

Johnny and his crime partner hid in the space between the roof and the sheet rock ceiling. Five cops entered the store. They were unaware that the criminals were still there hiding out. Johnny waited anxiously, hoping that he would not be discovered.

The officers brought two police dogs into the premises. The dogs immediately started barking just below the spot where the burglars were hiding. When Johnny heard one of the officers cock his shotgun, he knew the gig was up.

"I give up," Johnny shouted. "I'm not armed. I'm coming down."

Johnny jumped to the ground. The police dogs both attacked him, biting savagely at his legs and arms. He sustained serious injuries and had to be hospitalized.

Johnny was charged with breaking and entering and second degree burglary. He was a career criminal with an extensive rap sheet. He was facing a life sentence under California's Three Strikes and You're Out initiative. While awaiting trial, he contemplated his life of crime.

Johnny Alverez's criminality was rooted in a dysfunctional upbringing. Johnny was born and raised in a Mexican ghetto neighborhood in Florence, a region of Los Angeles. He was one of a dozen kids. His mother was an alcoholic and a cocaine dealer who used drugs and alcohol throughout her pregnancies. Johnny barely knew his father, because his father was usually in prison. Gangs were a way of life in the Alverez family. Johnny's father, his uncles, his five brothers, and even three of his sisters were gang members.

Johnny's childhood could be described in two words: criminal negligence. He was hungry and on his own most of his young life. The only time he got a decent meal was once a month when his mother received her welfare checks and bought hamburgers. His hand-me-down clothes were rarely washed and were riddled with holes and tears. During his preschool years, Johnny witnessed his brothers and sisters shooting up dope and having sex. Several times he walked in on his mother while she was having sex with various men.

His friend's house became a place of refuge. Johnny's most cherished childhood memories are of his friend's mother feeding him, bathing him, washing his clothes, and caring for him. Whenever he would visit, she would hug him and say, "You are okay, Johnny." His friend's family often went to Disneyland, the movies, or out to dinner, and Johnny would think, *I want to go.* Yet, no one in Johnny's family ever took him anywhere special. His family's attitude was, "Johnny is moving and talking. He must be all right."

He wasn't all right. The neglect caused deep emotional wounds that would dictate the course of Johnny's life.

When Johnny was nine years old, his mother came home late one night from a bar with one of her drug addict female friends. Johnny was sitting on the couch watching TV. After Johnny's mother went to sleep, her friend sat on the couch next to Johnny. She played with his penis and put his hand on her crotch. Johnny had seen so much sexual activity in the house over the years that he thought what she was doing was normal.

Johnny's mother was an alcoholic who went to the bars nearly every night. Johnny began sleeping on the couch in nothing but his boxers, hoping that his mother's drug addict friends would come home with her. A couple of times a week a drugged out friend would accompany her home and play with Johnny after his mother went to sleep. This abuse went on for several years. Of course, Johnny wasn't aware that he was being abused. He looked forward to the late night affection and was disappointed whenever his mother returned alone from the bars.

When Johnny was eleven years old he was in front of his house trying to shoot birds with a BB gun. A police patrol car drove down the street. Throughout his childhood Johnny had heard his family members disparage cops. Johnny took aim at the cop car and fired. The BB hit the rear window. The officers turned on their flashing lights and sirens and then pulled a u-turn. Johnny ran into his house. Moments later, the police arrived along with two back-up units. Five cops raided the house. Johnny's parents were not at home. He was cuffed and arrested.

Johnny was taken to Juvenile Hall. He was afraid, not knowing what would happen there. A counselor took his clothes and gave him a bright orange jumpsuit to wear. It smelled terrible and had disgusting stains all over it. Johnny was given a bedroll that contained one sheet, a pillow case, and an itchy wool blanket. Then he was locked in a holding cage.

Later, Johnny was directed into a dorm that housed a dozen other kids, ages 13-17. Johnny was the youngest boy in the dorm. He entered with his head held high, suppressing fear that was so overwhelming that he felt like vomiting. He went to his assigned bunk thinking, *I'll be okay, I'll be out tonight.* He was wrong on both counts.

Three Mexican gang members approached Johnny. One of the kids asked, "Where you from, fish?"

"Florence," Johnny answered, unsure why the kid had called him "fish."

"Fuck Florence," the kid replied in a challenging tone.

Johnny was tongue-tied.

One of the other boys said, "He just disrespected your 'hood, fool. What are you gonna do about it?"

Silence. Johnny was so scared he almost cried. He was only eleven. The three gang members were at least fifteen years old.

Smack! One of the kids cracked Johnny on the side of the head with an open hand. Johnny's eyes welled up with tears.

"He's gonna cry," one of the gang members said.

"There's no crying in Juvie, punk," one of the other kids said as he punched Johnny in the stomach.

Johnny doubled over and gasped for breath. The three gang members started wailing on him, and Johnny endured the first butt-kicking of his life. Three counselors ran into the room and broke up the fight.

"You're going to the Box," one of the counselors said as he separated the boys.

"What's that?" Johnny asked, tears rolling down his face.

"It's the hole."

That night Johnny was insolated in a single-man cell. He had never felt so alone. He wept uncontrollably, promising himself that he would never get into trouble again.

When Johnny returned to the dorm room the next day, the gang kids beat him up again. Johnny was placed in a one-man cell where he remained for three months. Neither of his parents, nor any other family member visited once to see if he was all right.

The day Johnny returned home from Juvenile Hall he was confused and angry. No one came to pick him up. He had no money, so he had to walk 10 miles to get home. That evening Johnny walked into his mother's room and saw her snorting a line of cocaine off a mirror. Curious, he pressed his finger into the pile of cocaine and stuck it into his mouth when she wasn't looking. The cocaine made him feel hyper and energetic. His mother went to the bars that night as usual, locking the bedroom door on her way out. Johnny used a hacksaw blade to unhinge the latch. He searched his mother's room and found the cocaine. He did what his mom did. He snorted it. At first it hurt the inside of his nostrils and his forehead. Moments later he felt euphoric. He went back into his mother's room three more times that night to snort cocaine. It was the beginning of what would become a life-long drug addiction. When he became older, Johnny realized the reason that his mother went to the bars every night was because she was a coke dealer.

When he was 12 years old, Johnny was initiated into the Florence gang. Typically, the initiation involved being "jumped in" — being beaten up by the other gang members; but Johnny was offered a pass because so many of his family members were already in the gang. Johnny didn't want a pass; he actually wanted to fight one of the three kids who were designated to jump him in. Johnny landed a few shots, but ultimately the three older kids took him to the ground, where they beat him without mercy. One eye was black and swollen shut; one ear was purple and he lost his hearing for a month.

Johnny started hanging out with the Florence gang members. His three main partners were Green Eyes, Trouble, and Stranger. Gang activities for the young teenagers involved doing drugs, committing burglaries, and fighting with rival gangs. Johnny was desperate to prove his value to the group. He would do anything they asked of him, just to fit in. Whenever possible, he would steal money from his mother's room and take his new homies out to eat. For the first time in his life the people around him valued Johnny for who he was. Before going to bed at night Johnny would think about his homeboys and look forward to being with them the next day. He was happy that he had real friends.

One time Johnny stole an eight-ball of coke from his

mother's room and met up with several of his homeboys. Stranger had some pot. They decided to roll a "primo," which is a joint of marijuana with cocaine sprinkled on it.

A homeboy named Shady remarked, "You guys are wasting the coke."

"No way, fool. Primos are the bomb," Green Eyes replied.

"Have you tried freebasing yet?" Shady asked.

"What's that?" Johnny inquired.

"It's when you smoke pure cocaine. That's the ultimate high."

Johnny pulled out the remaining three grams of cocaine. "Let's smoke it."

"You can't smoke it like that," Shady instructed. "First we've got to rock it up." Shady took his homeboys through the process of using ether to remove all of the impurities from the cocaine. What remained was a small pile of cocaine rocks that are commonly referred to as "crack."

"You gotta smoke it out of a pipe," Shady explained. He pulled a crack pipe out of his pocket.

Johnny took a hit off the pipe, held in the smoke, and felt his brain go numb. A tingling sensation ran throughout his body, and Johnny drifted into a miraculous state of serenity. It was the most wonderful experience he had ever known. Yet, the sensational high only lasted for 60 seconds. When he came down, Johnny exclaimed, "*Wow*, I think I just had an orgasm." The other kids laughed.

The freebasing party lasted for three hours. When the cocaine was eventually gone, Johnny and his friends experienced intense cravings. They did not want to come down from their drug-induced high. Johnny and Shady burglarized a house with the intention of stealing some items they could trade for crack, but they got caught.

Johnny's second trip to Juvenile Hall was nothing like the first. He was 14-years old and he was an active gang member. He hung out with other teenagers from the Florence gang. Johnny was sentenced to one year in confinement in the Y.A. Johnny didn't have any Florence tattoos like the other kids, and none of the kids in the dorm knew how to tattoo. Johnny wanted to represent his neighborhood when he got to Y.A., so he took a razor blade and cut F-13 – signifying Florence 13th Street – across his stomach. Johnny was sent to a Y.A. facility named "Camp Rocky," located in the Tehachapi Mountains. The 100-man dorm was partitioned into four sections. The facility was secured with 15-foot-high fences topped with razor wire. An electric fence surrounded the facility to prevent escapes. It was truly a prison for youth offenders.

The inmates at Camp Rocky were required to attend school and have a job assignment, such as working in the kitchen or cleaning bathrooms. Some kids worked outside the facility cleaning parks and doing clean-up alongside freeways.

On Johnny's first day at Camp Rocky he went to the yard. Three Mexican kids from 18th Street, an enemy gang, approached him and asked, "Where are you from?"

As a new kid on the yard, Johnny expected to be challenged. He was anticipating trouble, and he found it. When Johnny answered, "Florence," the three 18th Street gang members jumped him. They took Johnny to the ground and kicked him repeatedly in the face before several counselors arrived to break up the fight. Johnny was hurt badly. He had bruises and cuts all over his face.

After spending three days in the hole, Johnny was returned to the dorm. He was relieved to meet four teenagers from the Florence gang.

A kid named Pollo saw the F-13 stenciled on Johnny's stomach and said, "What's up, homeboy? You look like somebody just opened a can of whoop-ass on your face."

"I got jumped on the yard by three *Vatos* from 18th Street."

"What? We are going to fuck them fools up," Pollo said. Then he yelled across the dorm, "Hey Gangster, get the other homies and come here."

Moments later Gangster arrived with Bugsy and Huero in tow. Pollo introduced Johnny, and then gave his homies the rundown on what happened to Johnny while they were at their job assignments.

"It's on," Gangster said, his lips curling into a smile. He loved to fight. "In the chow hall at dinner, we are going to rush them fools."

That evening the five Florence gang members stood together at the end of the chow hall line. Johnny identified the three 18th Street combatants, who were sitting together. Johnny was scared and nervous, but he was down for the mission.

"Here's the plan," Gangster said, barely able to contain his sense of excitement. "We're going to get our trays, walk over casually, and crack them fools in the heads. Nobody say a word, just bust 'em in the head with your tray and kick their fucking asses."

All of the Florence homies agreed, and they did just that. A melee ensued with the five Florence gang members beating the snot out of the three 18th Street gang members before the counselors broke it up.

As the kids were being cuffed, Pollo said to Johnny, who had a cut over his eye and blood running down his face, "You all right, homie?"

Johnny stood proud and smiled, "Hell yeah! We fucked them fools up."

The brawl in the chow hall was a pivotal moment for 14-year-old Johnny Alverez. For the first time in his life somebody had his back; somebody cared about him. He felt loved. He thought, *I'm a gangster. This is me. This is my real family. I want to be in prison.*

When Johnny and his homeboys were released from the hole, they prepared for another battle with the 18th Street gang. They went at it five on five in the bathroom, which was concealed from the counselors' direct view. This time the Florence kids had weapons – socks with metal locks inside. One of their opponents sustained a broken nose and another had his head split open, requiring 30 stitches. Johnny had 90 days added to his sentence, but he didn't care. Nothing was more important than being loyal to his homies.

When Johnny was finally released from Camp Rocky, he returned to his parents' home in Florence. Living next door was a 14-year-old girl named Liz. Johnny and Liz had sex and she got pregnant. Nine months later his son, Johnny Alverez, Jr. was born. Johnny didn't know anything about being a father. The concept of a father's responsibility was foreign to him. He didn't feel anything for his son. All Johnny cared about was gangbanging and doing drugs.

Johnny became addicted to rock cocaine. One afternoon he and his homeboy Bugsy were coming down off coke, their drug cravings intense. They were walking down the street, desperate to get high.

"Let's jack somebody," Johnny said.

"I'm with that," Bugsy agreed. "Hey, look at that *vato* in the Corvette. See those gold chains he's wearing? That's an 8-ball right there."

The Corvette was stopped at a red light, and the car window was down. Johnny ran to the car, reached into the window, and snatched the two gold chains. The startled driver grabbed Johnny's wrist, but Johnny jerked his arm out of the car, chains in hand.

Johnny and Bugsy ran down the street and past a police car that was moving in the opposite direction. The officers made a u-turn and pursued the two youths.

"Stop! Get down on the ground!" the officers yelled at the kids through their car's loudspeaker.

Johnny and Bugsy continued to run.

The boys cut down a narrow alleyway. The officers brought their car to a screeching stop and gave chase on foot. Johnny threw away the chains while he was running. He hopped a fence. One of the cops was right behind him. The police officer tackled Johnny in a homeowner's back yard. Johnny was handcuffed and brought back to the police car. Bugsy was already sitting low in the back seat. The man in the Corvette drove up moments later and reported to the police what had transpired. They retraced Johnny's steps and found the two gold chains. Johnny was busted for robbery and sentenced to a year in Y.A.

This time Johnny served his sentence at Camp Page, which was for older boys, ages 15 - 17. Camp Page was a fire camp, meaning the kids were required to assist firefighters, and it was operated with military discipline. Every morning at 5:00 a.m. the boys were awakened by the animated shouts of the counselors. "Get up! Get your candy-asses out of bed." The juvenile delinquents were required to exercise for an hour every morning prior to breakfast. Some of the training sessions were brutally difficult; the kids were required to carry fire-fighting gear and water jugs up steep hills. In addition to their school work, the kids learned how to use chainsaws to cut trees, and to fight fires.

Camp Page was exceptionally violent. During his first week at the camp Johnny saw a vicious riot between the CRIPS and Bloods, black street gangs who were now saturated throughout the prison system. The next week Johnny saw two Mexican boys jump a white kid who had a blade. He sliced one of the Mexicans in the face. Johnny had never seen such a profusion of blood, and he was afraid. That night he prayed and asked God, "Please help me."

Johnny kept a sharpened pencil as a weapon with him at all times. He thought that if he stabbed the biggest kid in camp, nobody would mess with him. He decided to carry out his plan. The biggest kid at Camp Page was an enormous Mexican boy named Diablo. He was a man-child; a gargantuan 17-year-old boy who already had a full-brush mustache. Johnny studied Diablo's habits. He recognized that the big kid was most vulnerable when he exited the shower, wearing only a pair of sandals. Johnny waited for an opportune moment. Then he ambushed him. Johnny stabbed Diablo three times in the stomach and in the side. A counselor saw the attack, and Johnny was punished.

Johnny was banished to the hole for two weeks. When he returned to the yard, his Florence homeboys treated him like a conquering hero. Teenagers from the MS and 38th Street gangs formed an alliance with the Florence gang. Johnny was viewed as a leader. The other kids shared their cigarettes and drugs with Johnny, and he relished the attention.

At Camp Page Johnny also had a confrontation with Danny Boy, an immense Samoan teenager who was the leader of the CRIPS gang. Danny Boy usually picked on smaller kids. Johnny wanted to be recognized as a tough guy who would stand up for his homies. He confronted Danny Boy on the yard, where everybody would see the fight.

"Why you always disrespecting my homies?" Johnny challenged, eager to engage the bigger kid.

Danny Boy shot him a murderous stare and responded, "Fuck you and your faggot-assed homeboys. You ain't gonna do nothing about it and you know it."

Fearless as a gladiator, Johnny reached into his back pocket, grabbed an ink pen, and stabbed the giant Samoan in the side.

"Mother fucker!" Danny Boy screamed. "I'm going to kill you."

Johnny stabbed him two more times before Danny Boy knocked the pen out of his hand.

An alarm sounded. "Get down!" commanded a counselor over the loudspeaker.

All across the yard teenagers hit the dirt. Danny Boy glared at Johnny, wild-eyed and possessed. Johnny made a headlong charge at Danny Boy attempting to tackle his opponent to the ground. It was like slamming into a cinder block wall. Danny Boy flung Johnny to the ground. With maniacal fury, Danny Boy unleashed a barrage of punches. Johnny withered under the ruthless assault. He took shot after shot to the face.

Three counselors arrived to break up the fight. They pulled Danny Boy away, but the Samoan possessed extraordinary strength. He tossed the grown men aside and turned his titanic rage back to Johnny, who was dazed and flat on his back.

Danny Boy kicked Johnny in the side with all his might, breaking two ribs. Then he unleashed another series of brain-rattling punches to Johnny's face. Johnny was powerless against the relentless onslaught. His face was a bloody mess.

The three counselors pulled cans of mace from their belts and sprayed each of the boys in the face. Danny Boy and Johnny both screamed as the mace burned their eyes, temporarily blinding them. The counselors cracked both boys several times with their nightsticks. They were subdued, handcuffed, and taken to the hole.

The stabbing incidents resulted in Johnny's sentence being extended six months. He didn't care whether he was incarcerated or on the streets. Either way he was kicking it with his Florence homeboys; the ones he believed really cared about him. Twenty additional years would pass before Johnny finally realized that the love he thought he felt from his homies was really just an illusion.

It was never the love he so desperately craved.

Johnny was 17 years old when he was released from Camp Page. The first thing he did was hook up with Liz…and get her pregnant again.

Johnny wasn't free long enough to see the birth of his daughter, Fernanda. For his next crime Johnny decided to rob a car wash. He pulled a gun on the cashier and demanded, "Give me the money." The cashier complied. Johnny stuffed the money into his pockets. He raced out of the car wash and came face-to-face with two police officers who were pointing their guns straight at him. They had watched and waited while the crime went down. Johnny wasn't just one of "America's Dumbest Criminals," he was also one of its unluckiest.

"Freeze, dumbass," the officer ordered. "Put down the weapon and lie flat on the ground."

Johnny followed the officer's instructions. He was busted again. He was put in a section of the jail reserved for juveniles who commit serious crimes. Johnny's public defender was able to negotiate a two-year sentence in the adult state prison system for an armed robbery charge. Johnny remained in the L.A. County Jail until his 18th birthday, at which time he was transferred to the "Big House." Despite the fact that Johnny had once looked forward to the day he would enter a real prison, he was now petrified.

Johnny's first stop was the Reception Center at Chino, where inmates underwent a 90-day evaluation. He discovered that prison was quite different than Y.A. He learned that all the Southern California Mexican gang members banded together in prison and were called "Suranos." Mexicans from Northern California ran with the Blacks and were known as "Northanos." Mexicans from the Fresno area were called the "Fresno Bulldogs." Hispanic men who came from south of the border – Mexico, Central America and South America – were known as "Pisas." Johnny was warned by other Suranos that the Northanos and Fresno Bulldogs were their enemies, and that sometimes Pisas could be enemies, as well.

In a rare moment of clarity, Johnny saw how ridiculous the Mexican gang culture had become. On the streets of L.A., Mexican gang members from 18th Street, Watts, Florence, MS, and other neighborhoods shot and killed one another. Yet, when they came to prison, they were all Suranos, who fought together against other Mexicans from different regions. The entire Mexican gang subculture was fragmented and made no sense. For Johnny, the insights were fleeting; he was confident he would never turn his back on his Florence homeboys. If they were Suranos, he was a Surano. He was down for the cause.

Johnny was soon transferred to the prison at Susanville, California, where he learned what being a Surano was really about. One week after he arrived, the Suranos, who were also known as Southsiders, were involved in a territorial dispute with the Northanos over which gang would control a concrete table on the yard. There were seven tables on the yard. Three were controlled by the Northanos and the Black CRIPS they ran with; only one was controlled by the Southsiders, who were demanding equality. Negotiations were at a standstill.

The shotcaller from the Southsiders decided that the only way to get the table was to take it by force. An ambush was planned by the Southsiders. On the day of the planned attack, Johnny was ordered to bring four shanks to the yard. This meant that Johnny would be required to "keester" the makeshift knives – to wrap them in cellophane and hide them inside his asshole. Johnny was aghast, but he did it because he needed to prove that he was a down homie.

The Southsiders' ambush took place on the "weight pile," the place on the yard where the inmates lifted weights. Johnny was a youngster, so he was required to be on the front line of the assault. The melee began when one of the Suranos stabbed the Northanos shotcaller in the neck. The most frightening five minutes of Johnny's entire life then ensued. Men were stabbed, cracked in the head with dumbbells, and shot by the guards. When the chaos finally ended, ambulances arrived to transport many of the combatants to the hospital. Johnny was fortunate in that he was not badly injured.

During the subsequent lockdown, Johnny's roommate introduced him to "slamming" heroin. "Slamming" is prison slang for intravenous drug use. Compared to the monotony of being in a small cage 24 hours a day, Johnny's experience with heroin was similar to being out of prison, free on furlough. After vomiting several times, his mind drifted to faraway places. In his drug-induced state, Johnny's mind was free from the oppression of prison life. From that point on, Johnny associated drug use with a sense of freedom. It did not matter whether it was heroin, coke, or pot; Johnny just wanted to get high, numb the pain of incarceration, and feel good. To acquire drugs Johnny did whatever the big homies required him to do. He'd make weapons, hold their drug stashes — even stab someone. Johnny became a slave to drugs and the gangbanging lifestyle.

Upon his release from the Big House, Johnny returned to his parents' house. He reconnected with Liz and got her pregnant for the third time. It did not occur to Johnny that he was doing the identical thing to Liz that his father had done to his mother. Anyway, he didn't care about Liz or the children he sired.

Johnny had only been free for two weeks when his parole agent arrived at his house for a surprise inspection. The parole agent found marijuana and an "outfit" — a hypodermic needle that he used for slamming heroin. Johnny was handcuffed and sent back to prison for six months for a parole violation.

By the time Johnny was released from prison, his entire body was covered with tattoos. On the day of his release, a carload of his Florence homies saw him standing in his front yard.

"What's up, dog?" Green Eyes, one of his childhood homeboys, called out. "You want to get loaded?"

"You know it."

Just like that, Johnny was destined for further self-destruction. The homies got Johnny high and then they got him laid. Once again, he felt the false sense of love and belonging that would always prove to be his downfall. The homies also got him busted. Within a week they were arrested for vehicular theft. Johnny had no idea the car was stolen, but that was irrelevant. He returned to prison for another year for violating his parole.

After serving another stint in the clink, Johnny returned to his home in Florence, as he always did. His gang life became increasingly more dangerous and extreme. One afternoon, rival gang members did a drive-by shooting on Johnny's house. The gangsters leaned out of their car window and opened fire with semi-automatic weapons. Lisa, Johnny's nine-year-old sister, was shot in the leg. Johnny and his brother took her to the hospital. While the doctors attended to Lisa, the Alverez brothers plotted revenge. They suspected that the drive-by shooters were from the Watts gang, but they were unsure. Johnny infiltrated the Watts neighborhood, started dating a girl whose brother was in the gang, and pumped her for information. He learned the identity of the culprits and where they could be found.

The Watts gang members hung out in an alleyway behind a liquor store. Along with his brother, Marko, and a homeboy named Stranger, Johnny sought to retaliate one evening. The three Florence gang members drove slowly down the alley.

"Look," said Stranger, who was driving. "That's them kicking it on the hoods of those two low-riders."

"Mother fucker! I count twelve," Marko responded. He pulled out his pistol. "I brought the wrong gun. This piece of shit only holds six slugs. Johnny, what are you working with?"

"I got a 44 Magnum. Six bullets," Johnny replied.

"Six for you and six for me, we are going to fuck them fools up, pero."

Johnny did not share Marko's enthusiasm for the revenge mission. Fear and apprehension dominated his thought process.

Johnny observed, "I guarantee you, they are strapped. We got to handle our business and get the fuck out of here as fast as we can."

Stranger studied the configuration of the alleyway as he inched their car forward. The alley came to a dead-end about 50 meters beyond the point where their enemies' cars were parked.

"Look, homies," Stranger cautioned as he pointed toward the dead end. "I'm going to have to flip a bitch down there. You need to shoot them on the way back up the alley; otherwise we could get trapped."

"Yeah, I see that," Marko replied. "Punch it. Let's get busy."

Stranger pressed the accelerator and the car moved quickly down the alleyway. When they passed the Watts gang members' cars, Johnny stared at his enemies. His eyes locked onto a young man who was holding a beer. The recognition was instantaneous. Johnny looked back and saw manic activity around the two cars. The 12 Watts gang members were preparing to do battle.

"Look homie, them fools know what's up." Johnny's heart was beating wildly. "Fuck, this is serious. Hurry up, Stranger. We have to move before they get their guns."

Too late. At that very moment the Watts gang members were retrieving their weapons and assuming defensive positions. By the time that the Florence gang members reached the end of the alley and turned around, they recognized that their enemies were combat ready and waiting.

"Un-fucking believable!" Marko exclaimed from the back seat.

"I'm going to punch it," Stranger hollered as he hit the gas with full force. "Kill them fools."

As they raced past the Watts gang members, Johnny leaned out of the passenger side window in the front seat brandishing his 44 Magnum. Marko did the same from the rear seat. They both opened fire. Seconds later bullets were whizzing back at them. Clank! Clank! Clank! Clank! Several bullets rattled into the side of the car.

The Florence gang members sped away. Johnny stuck his head out the window and looked back. He saw three Watts gangsters run out into the alley shooting at them. Another barrage of bullets slammed into their car. One of the bullets shattered through the rear window and into Johnny's ribs.

"Mother fuaaaaaaah!" he screamed as the bullet ripped through muscle and bone, tore away at Johnny's larynx, and lodged just half an inch above his heart. Searing pain burst inside Johnny's chest. "I think I'm going to die," he wanted to say but the words came out in an unintelligible garble. His vocal cords had been damaged and he couldn't speak.

"Jesus Christ!" Strange exclaimed when he saw Johnny's blood-soaked shirt.

Marko leaned over the back seat and looked at his brother's wound. "We have to get him to a hospital right away."

"Not before we ditch the guns," Stranger said. "You know the pigs will be there. That's how it is with gunshot wounds. Pigs gotta do a police report. If they notice the bullet holes and shattered rear window, they will search the car."

The Florence gang members stashed their guns under a dumpster and then took Johnny to a nearby hospital. Shortly after arriving at the hospital, Johnny was rushed into emergency surgery. Johnny was in critical condition for several weeks. Doctors later informed Johnny that it was a miracle he survived. He remained in the hospital for two full months. Doctors performed a second surgery to repair Johnny's vocal cords. Nine months would pass before he could speak again.

Despite nearly dying from the bullet wounds he sustained in the shootout with the Watts gang members, Johnny never considered relinquishing his attachment to his Florence homeboys. His favorite thing to do was to kick it at "the tracks" with the homies and slam speedballs, which are a combination of coke and heroin. The tracks where they hung out consisted of nothing more than a couple of old ratty couches that were situated under several shade trees near the railroad tracks. It was a semi-secluded spot where the Florence gangsters went to do drugs and have sex with girls at night.

One evening Johnny and Green Eyes were at the tracks slamming speedballs. A train came by and in one of the boxcars were two armed men from a rival gang. When the train passed the spot, the two men started shooting at Johnny and Green Eyes. They were so high that instead of ducking for cover they started laughing. The fun ended when Johnny took a bullet to the knee, and Green Eyes took one in the shoulder. The wounds were excruciatingly painful, but not life-threatening.

Johnny's gang life was filled with death and disaster. He was shot on two other occasions. One time Johnny and his friend Alex were in front of Alex's house, washing the car, when they became the victims of another drive-by shooting. Three rival gang members shot at them with double-barreled shotguns. Alex was shot in the knee and the thigh; Johnny was shot in the ankle.

Another time Johnny was with 20 of his Florence homeboys at Huntington Park, where they met an equal number of men from the Slain gang. The objective of the meeting was to reach a truce that would end hostilities and drive-by shootings.

Unfortunately, cooler heads could not prevail. The rival gangs began fighting. The melee that began with bats and knives ended in a deadly shootout. Johnny was one of seven gang members who were shot that day; a bullet grazed the top of his head. He also sustained a broken nose when he was hit in the face with a baseball bat. He has no idea how many Slain gang members were shot or killed.

On three separate occasions Johnny's homies were murdered in his presence. One homeboy was shot three times and died in his arms. Another was shot in the head at a shootout and died instantly. The third was a homegirl who was shot six times in a drive-by shooting. She died in the car on the way to the hospital.

Johnny's pattern of fighting with rival gangs, doing drugs, committing burglaries and robberies, and returning to prison with a new criminal conviction or parole violation was repeated for the next decade. He was serving life in prison on the installment plan. He was never free for more than four consecutive months.

Every time he was arrested he was incarcerated in the Los Angeles County Jail. As mentioned in Chapter One, the L.A. County Jail is one of the most violent places on the planet. It is particularly brutal for Mexican and Black gang members who are constantly at war with one another. During his many stays at the L.A. County Jail, Johnny participated in 20 separate race riots. He saw several men get stabbed in the throat, back, and stomach, and observed countless people get hurt, some fatally. His emotions ran the gamut of extreme pride after a victorious battle to loneliness and despondency when he was sitting in the hole nursing his wounds. Such is the life of a Mexican gang member.

Following his arrest for the rooftop burglaries, Johnny was facing a mandatory sentence of 25 years to life in state prison — life if he was found guilty of a third strike. He was fortunate to be offered a 12-year sentence in a plea bargain arrangement, wherein he would be required to serve 85 percent of his sentence.

Johnny participated in six separate race riots with the

Suranos during the first three years of his sentence. His record of ongoing violence resulted in him being transferred to the notorious Corcoran SHU (Security Housing Unit) described in Chapter One. Johnny arrived at the Corcoran SHU following the Gladiator Wars Trial of guards who were tried for murdering inmates. The guards were acquitted on the murder charges. At that time, the SHU was under Federal supervision. The inmates were isolated by race. As a result, Johnny's five-year SHU term was disciplinary free. Johnny's classification score was lowered every year. When he was released from the SHU, Johnny's classification score dropped from super-max security level four to a level three maximum security. He was transferred to Donavan State Prison in San Diego.

When Johnny arrived at Donavan, he experienced a period of culture shock. Most of the inmates at Donavan are "programmers," a term used to describe prisoners who attempt to remain disciplinary free. Johnny had never previously been to a prison where the Suranos were not at war with the convicts of other races or regions. At first he thought it was a prison for protective custody inmates. He felt out of place. When he was alone in his cell he considered stabbing someone so that he would be sent back to the SHU or a level four maximum security prison. However, Johnny only had two years remaining on his sentence, and he had the Three Strikes Law hovering above his head like a hangman's noose.

Johnny was assigned to a job working in the woodshop. There he met several down homies who had changed their lives. The men were attending Alcoholics Anonymous meetings, getting a GED or college degree, and attending church. Such positive opportunities were not available at the higher security level prisons, which had been Johnny's previous stops. There had been no freedom of choice. At most prisons in the State of California, Mexican convicts are required to live by a virulent, uncompromising code of conduct.

Johnny was invited to attend a meeting of Amity, the prison's drug rehabilitation program. At Amity, men participate in support groups where they share private and painful experiences. Johnny heard men describe being physically and sexually abused, express agonizing emotions, and saw them openly weep. He was appalled. *What a bunch of faggots,* he thought.

At the conclusion of the meeting, a black man hugged Johnny. He was disgusted and horrified. Hugging a black man at any of his previous prisons would get a Surano stabbed. Johnny shoved the man away.

The black guy was perplexed. He said, "I love you, man. You're my Amity brother."

"I don't even know you," Johnny responded. "If you ever try to touch me again I will stab you in the neck."

Johnny didn't want to return to Amity, but the down homies who had changed their lives continued to invite him and encouraged him to stop using drugs. Johnny admired the changes he saw in the other Southsiders. Despite a lifetime of negative conditioning, he felt a powerful desire to change his life, starting with the Amity meetings. For the next month Johnny regularly attended meetings. He did not interact much at first; he mostly sat at the back of the room and listened as the other men took turns describing how drug addiction had destroyed their lives. His feelings were all over the place. One minute he would be listening to a man share a painful truth and think, *what a buster. It ain't right for a homie to tell family secrets.* Moments later, someone would describe something that Johnny went through as a child, and he thought he might cry. *What's the matter with me?* He thought. *Men are not supposed to cry in front of other men.*

Later that same evening, Johnny experienced a profound transformation. He was alone in his cell reflecting on the stories he had heard that day at Amity. He started crying for the first time since he was in Juvenile Hall at age eleven. Painful emotions poured out of him in gasping, raging torrents. Johnny could not control the tears that flowed from his eyes, nor did he want to. Driven by a profound, instinctual need for salvation, Johnny went to his knees and prayed for the first time in his life.

"God, please help me," he cried out between sobs. "Please take this sickness away. Please God, take away my desire to slam dope. Please God, I don't want to be like this anymore. I want to change."

Following the prayer, Johnny lay on his bunk and felt relief. For the first time in his life he felt peaceful inside. In that halcyon moment, he knew that God had answered his prayer. He thought, *I'm ready now.*

The next morning Johnny went to Amity. Other men approached him and remarked that they saw a glow in his face. Johnny found the courage to stand before the group and share his pain. He spoke about how he was neglected by his parents, about the sexual abuse with the alcoholic women, and the remorse he felt for all of the people he had harmed. As Johnny expelled his internal demons, he came apart again. He wept openly in front of the group, and was surprised when one of the down homies approached him with tears streaming down his face. The man hugged Johnny fiercely and said, "Let it out homie. I'm here for you."

The genuine words of care and support brought comfort to Johnny's wounded soul. His body shook as he cried without restraint. When Johnny finally regained his composure, the other Mexican men in the group took turns hugging him. The white men and black men followed. Johnny was amazed by their unbridled support and that his own prejudice had completely disappeared. A mysterious, invisible force moved through Johnny and brought deliverance to him from a lifetime of heartache. The stigmas of his past were all washed away.

During the months that followed, Johnny began to attend church regularly. He had always believed in God; however, now he wanted to study God's word and live by God's laws. He learned to embrace people of other races and cry in front of people without feeling shame. From the men he met at church, Johnny discovered a love he had never known — unconditional love. He realized that the love he thought he felt all those years from his homeboys wasn't genuine love at all. It was only acceptance for a kid who was vulnerable and desperate to be loved by anybody. He also perceived that he wasn't the gangster he thought he was. He realized that deep down he was weak. He now expresses his feelings and has love in his heart, and he cares about others. Johnny realized that throughout his gangster life he was living in darkness. Now he sees the light.

As I write these words, Johnny is scheduled for release from prison in one week. This time will be different. He is a changed man. Johnny had been clean and sober for two years. He plans to reside in a sober living home that is sponsored by the Victory Outreach Church. One of the things he is truly looking forward to is returning to Florence, where he intends to visit the schools he attended and speak to young gang members. His goal is to deter youths from making the same mistakes that he made.

What To Expect When You Join A Gang
- Rival gangs will attempt to kill you
- Police will harass you constantly and arrest you
- The gang always comes first
- You will be obligated to fight, stab, and shoot people every day
- You must be alert and be prepared to be attacked at any time
- You will engage in illegal and dangerous activities that will eventually land you in prison
- People will hate you
- No one will trust you
- You will place your loved ones in danger
- Your house will be shot at
- You will cause your family immense sorrow and worry
- You will not be allowed to express your real feelings
- The gang will control every aspect of your life
- You will adopt your friends' bad habits
- You will become addicted to all kinds of drugs
- You will not be allowed to make your own choices because a shotcaller will always tell you what to do
- You cannot ever take your little brother or sister to a park
- You cannot have a regular job because your rivals will recognize you

CHAPTER 10
The Gentlemen Bank Robber & Developing Self-Esteem

From my participation in CROP I learned that the two biggest issues at-risk adolescents face are gangs and substance abuse. While speaking with these kids, I have also discovered that low self-esteem is the primary reason they join gangs, use drugs or alcohol, and engage in criminal activities. To illustrate this point, I'd like to begin this segment by telling you the story of Joe Jackson, a CROP member the FBI dubbed as "The Gentleman Bank Robber."

Joe Jackson was born with a speech impediment that caused him to stutter. In school, the other kids mimicked Joe and made fun of him. When his classmates laughed at his stuttering, Joe felt terrible about himself. He was afraid to speak to anyone or get involved in peer activities.

When he was 13 years old, Joe's older sister's friend gave him a beer. Joe quickly discovered that intoxication took away his fear of interacting with others. He found that he enjoyed marijuana even more than beer, and began to hang around with a group of kids who smoked pot daily before and after school. In order to gain acceptance into the group, Joe began stealing money from his mother's purse to pay for the pot. Whenever he had marijuana, the others kids wanted to hang out with him and his popularity rose.

At the age of 16, Joe discovered his first true love— cocaine. Nothing made Joe feel better than getting high on coke, yet he had no way to pay for the drug. He awoke a sleeping giant. He started committing burglaries to get the money he needed to support his drug habit. At his lowest point, Joe backed a large truck up to his parents' home and stole everything. Despite the despicable things that he had done, Joe's parents still cared about him. They paid for Joe to attend several drug rehabilitation centers. Over a five-year period Joe was in and out of seven different rehab clinics. He tried everything from a 30-day outpatient program to an intensive, nine-month in-house clinical program. Nothing worked.

It was during one of his rehab stints that Joe met a man named Kyle. Kyle robbed banks. Kyle explained that only about 60 percent of bank robberies were solved and that bank tellers were trained to do whatever the robbers demanded. Joe learned that first-time offenders were usually sentenced to five years or less, provided they did not use a weapon. Joe felt that he could pull off a bank robbery.

Prior to his first bank robbery, Joe was scared to death. His solution was to get loaded. He purchased a hat, glasses, and a fake moustache with which to disguise himself, and used a taxi as the getaway driver. The taxi was parked only a block away. He gave the driver $20 and told him he'd be back in five minutes.

Joe chose a Bank of America that was close to a freeway onramp, because he anticipated that stoplights might be a problem. He went in the morning when there were not many customers. The teller was a middle-aged black man.

"Hi Sir," said the teller. "How can I help you?"

Joe simply handed him a note which read: "Bank robbery. I want all of the $20's, $50's and $100's in the top two drawers. No GPS transponders or dye packs. Remember your training." Kyle had informed Joe that most of the robbers who got caught were unaware of the GPS transponders and the dye packs that exploded a cloud of blue powder, or that the tellers had a silent alarm button under the counter that alerted the nearest police department.

The teller read the note twice, apparently in disbelief. Then, slowly and deliberately, he began to stack the 100's, 50's, and 20's.

Before leaving Joe said, "Please don't hit the alarm until after I'm out the door. Thank you."

His courteous nature earned him the Gentleman Bank Robber nickname from the FBI.

Joe calmly walked out the door, and then sprinted all the way to the taxi. He instructed the driver to get on the freeway and heard the sirens of a police car as he made his getaway. Joe could not believe how easy it was, or how smoothly it had gone. He made off with $8,000 that day and felt confident that he could rob a bank any time he needed some quick cash. His next two bank robberies were also executed flawlessly, earning Joe $5,000 and $12,000 respectively.

Joe went to Vegas, where he indulged in booze, gambling, drugs, and whores. By now his cocaine addiction was completely out of control. He was even using a needle. He had been shooting up for days when he ran out of money and decided to rob his fourth bank. He chose one that was adjacent to a freeway onramp and used his familiar pattern of hiring a taxi for the getaway car. However, this time things did not go according to plan.

The teller was a heavy-set white woman in her 50's. At first she deliberately delayed Joe by moving very slowly. Then she put the bait money on the counter with the rest to the money, but Joe spotted the GPS transponder. He became angry and threw the money stack at the teller. Everyone in the bank stared at Joe, and he realized that he needed to make a break for it.

He grabbed the money from the counter and took off. The bank had a set of double doors. Joe got through the first door, but could not get the second door to open. He panicked. He feared that he was caught between the two doors. Desperate, he lowered his shoulder, banging into the door. Money flew everywhere. Joe did not realize that the second door would not open until the first door had closed all the way. He thought that he was trapped. Just when he resigned himself to being caught, someone opened the outside door. Joe bolted through the opening and took off. He made it to the taxi and was hopeful that no one had seen him running from the bank. He was lucky. It was a close call, but Joe thought he was going to get away.

Joe instructed the taxi driver to take the freeway; however, they got stuck in traffic. The police responded quickly to the bank's alarm. Within minutes a half-dozen police cars appeared. The officers got out of their cars and drew their guns. Joe was really trapped this time.

"Come out with your hands up," one of the police officers ordered.

The taxi driver was frightened. When he opened his door to

get out of the cab, Joe flew out of the door on the other side of the car and took off running through traffic. A couple of city construction workers tried to detain him. Joe was able to break free from their grasp, but they slowed him enough for one of the cops to close the gap. The officer tackled him from behind. Joe fought to get away, but was ultimately subdued by several cops.

Joe pled guilty to the four bank robberies and signed a plea bargain agreement for five years in federal prison. When Joe was released, he only stayed straight for three months. He was at a party one evening and thought that it would be okay if he drank a few beers. It wasn't, of course. The gateway to his intense desire to do coke had been opened. The sleeping giant in Joe's head re-awakened. Joe quickly discovered that when an addict relapses, the cravings are 10-times as bad. He simply could not get enough cocaine. Once again he turned to bank robberies to get the money required to feed the sleeping giant.

As before, Joe got caught, as most criminals usually do. Joe pled guilty and signed another five-year plea-bargain agreement. During his second stint in federal prison, Joe made a personal commitment to turn his life around. He took a mail order course to become a personal fitness trainer.

Following his release from prison the second time, Joe got his act together. He passed the test to become a personal trainer and got a job at Bally's Gym. It did not last. This time it was marijuana use that opened the gateway to Joe's desire for harder drugs. He started using cocaine again, and his life quickly fell apart. Joe went on another run of cocaine addiction and bank robberies. He robbed eight banks before getting caught. The laws had changed since Joe's last conviction; a bank robbery was no longer a federal crime. This time Joe was prosecuted in California, where he would be facing a 25-year to life sentence under the Three Strikes law. He pled guilty to all eight counts and threw himself on the mercy of court. This was a risky move in a state where men are routinely given sentences of 25 years to life for petty crimes, such as stealing a piece of pizza. As a result of his obvious drug addiction, the judge did show him a slight degree of mercy by sentencing him to 25 years without the life top. He would be required to serve 85 percent of the sentence.

Joe's story is important because it provides a dramatic example of how the gateway drugs—alcohol and marijuana—can lead to the use of hard drugs and destroy someone's life. His story is also important because it illustrates how low self-esteem during adolescence can lead someone astray. Unfortunately, Joe's story is not uncommon. Many things can happen to a kid that lead to low self-esteem. For Joe, it was the relentless teasing from other kids because of his stuttering. For Johnny Alverez, it was neglect by his parents. For Diego Jones, it was the bullying from the 18th Street gang members. For Rodwick Johnson, it was his mother's physical abusiveness. For Tim Harris, it was parental abandonment and the corporal punishment of his foster mother. Kids with low self-esteem rooted in parental abuse act out against authority and lash out at others in anger. Kids rejected by their peers do stupid things in an effort to gain the approval of others. Kids with low self-esteem drink and do drugs because they are trying to mask painful emotions and think it will make them feel better about themselves. The real reason a teenage boy joins a gang is because he is looking for a feeling of belonging. The real reason a teenage girl shoplifts clothes, jewelry or make-up is because she feels inadequate about her appearance and is seeking approval from her peers. In *The Seven Habits of Highly Successful People,* Stephen Covey pinpoints the reason why teenagers become involved in anti-social behavior.

If we do not develop our own self awareness, we empower other people to shape our lives by default. We reactively live the scripts handed to us by associates, other people's agendas. These scripts come from people not principles. And they rise out of our deep vulnerabilities, our deep dependency on others, and our needs for acceptance and love, for belonging, for a sense of importance and worth, for a feeling that we matter. [1]

In *The Psychology of Winning,* Denis Waitley defines self-esteem as, "the value you place on yourself." [2] With this in mind, I compiled a list of the different ways in which the other CROP members and the kids I met through the program were devalued. These triggers for low self-esteem include:

- Being targeted by rumors, gossip, or name calling
- Subjected to bullying, even cyber-bullying where people taunt them over the Internet
- Belief that they are unwanted or unloved by one or more parent
- Feeling ashamed because of the way they look
- Feeling stupid because they do poorly in school
- Have lost parents through divorce or suicide or abandonment
- Have parents who physically or verbally abused them
- Have parents who showed favoritism to a sibling
- Believed and internalized the worst criticism and opinions of others

In the book *The Transformation Power of Crisis,* psychotherapist Dr. Robert Alter suggests that healing and growth cannot occur without that moment of self-realization when the kids and parents discover the emotional wounds that the kids carry within them that caused the anti-social behavior.

None of us can grow unless we spend some time in the past figuring out what happened that keeps influencing how we are today. That time in our lives is like an electrical generating station that keeps feeding tremendous power into the repetitive and destructive patterns of thoughts, feelings and behavior in our present lives. The essence of addiction to all mood altering drugs is the attempt to feel positive emotions instead of the negative ones we're feeling at the moment. [3]

Joe's cocaine addiction was deeply rooted in the traumatic events from the relentless teasing he endured as a kid. He was constantly searching for acceptance and trying to overcome the negative emotions and pain he held deep within. All he wanted to do was feel good.

When it comes to helping a child overcome the problem of low self-esteem, Dr. Alter instructs:

> **The best way to remove the steel plate of low self-esteem is to wear it down with repeated messages of praise, gratitude, appreciation, admiration and love. Use every opportunity to commend him, tell him he's good, tell him he's wonderful, tell him you like him, and tell him you love him.[4]**

Dr. Alter's insights resonated with a story that Dr. Wayne Dyer told about the Bamimba tribe in Africa on his PBS television special *The Power of Intention*. The story suggests a novel approach to criminal rehabilitation that I believe the youth justice system and all parents should consider.

> **In the Bamimba tribe of South Africa when someone commits a serious crime a ceremony is held. The entire tribe gathers in a circle with the person who committed the crime standing in the middle. Then one at a time every member of the tribe takes turns affirming the criminal's value. They remind him of all good things that he has done in his lifetime, his good deeds, positive attributes, and personal strengths. No one is allowed to speak badly about him in any way. They only talk about his acts of kindness and the wonderful things about him. Then, after every possible positive comment has been made, he is welcomed back into the tribe.[5]**

There is great wisdom in the Bamimba tribe's approach to criminal rehabilitation. They clearly understand that the best way to help someone turn his life around is by affirming his value to society and rebuilding his self-esteem.

Once I understood that low self-esteem was the primary reason that adolescents become involved in anti-social behavior, I began to engage the teenagers I met at CROP in a different way. I started asking them questions related to their self-worth and found that the most troubled kids responded in terms of how their peers defined them. It seemed as though their self-images were based primarily on what they believed the other kids thought about them. They also measured themselves based on their appearance, their sense of style, their social status, and their peer group. The kids would say things such as, "I'm a geek," "I'm ugly," "I'm a stoner," or "I'm a gang member." I wanted to encourage these teenagers to stop defining themselves based on the opinions of others, but found that I was ill-equipped to do so. This led me to seek out and collect information about developing self-esteem. The information was condensed into the following 10-step program for building self-esteem:

Step 1: Start an "accomplishments scorecard." Write down everything that you have accomplished in your lifetime; things like learning how to ride a bike, playing an instrument, or getting good grades on a test in school. By recalling previous accomplishments you gain the self-confidence required to do new things.

Step 2: Get involved in after school activities where you can express your passions and natural talents and make friends based on common interested and common goals.

Step 3: Surround yourself with people who appreciate your unique qualities. Disassociate yourself from people who are constantly criticizing you or putting you down. Avoid people who express pessimism about your hopes and dreams.

Step 4: Find a mentor. Whatever your dream may be, you can find a person who has already achieved a similar goal. Identify that person and write them a heartfelt letter. Tell them about your dreams and ask if they would offer advice in the form of a half-hour monthly phone call. Most successful people love to share their knowledge.

Step 5: Read books concerning your hopes and dreams. When you read a biography about someone who has accomplished the goals that you are pursuing, you become inspired. And when you read "How To" books you learn the tricks of the trade.

Step 6: Affirm the self-esteem of others by recognizing their finest qualities. One of my favorite exercises for developing self-esteem is to title a piece of paper: "What I Like About You." Then write down everything you like about a friend or family member, and give it to them as a gift. You will be amazed by the response. The gift of appreciation is one of the most special things you can give to another human being.

Step 7: Get involved in some kind of community service activity. There is no better tool for building self-esteem than serving others, particularly those in need. This can be as simple as helping your little brother or sister with their homework.

Step 8: Believe in your divinity. Every religion and every spiritual tradition throughout the world teaches that human beings were molded in the image of our Creator. Believe that you are a child of God. As such, you are perfect just the way you are.

Step 9: Believe in yourself. Remember, self-esteem is the value you place on yourself. Choose to believe in yourself. Choose to believe that you can accomplish any goal that you set out to achieve. Don't worry about what other people think about your chances of success.

Step 10: Make a lifetime commitment to your personal development. Read books. Listen to inspirational audio programs. Attend lectures and seminars. Take classes at the Learning Annex or a local college. The more you learn, the more your self-esteem will grow.

CHAPTER 11
Overzealous Prosecution

*U*SA *Today* documented 201 cases in which judges determined that Justice Department prosecutors violated laws or ethical rules. The judges blasted prosecutors for abuses that put innocent people in prison. They caught prosecutors hiding evidence, lying to judges and juries, breaking plea bargains, covering up evidence that could've discredited accusers, failing to turn over evidence to defendants, offering reduced sentences to convicted felons in exchange for lying to juries and coaching witnesses.

"*USA Today* found a pattern of serious, glaring misconduct," said Pace University law professor Bennett Gershman, an expert on misconduct by prosecutors. "It's systematic now, and the system is not able to control this type of behavior. There is no accountability. None of the offending prosecutors were punished. Prosecutors deliberately cut corners to win. They are often motivated by personal ambition or partisan reasons."[1]

The foregoing information was extracted from an article titled "Prosecutors Can Tip the Scale" that appeared on the front page of *USA Today* on September 23, 2010 by Brad Heath and Kevin McCoy. In America, we are raised to believe we have the world's best criminal justice system. This is simply not true. The *USA Today* article reveals that many prosecutors are self-centered rascals who only care about one thing: their conviction rate. The system breeds a "convict at all costs mentality" that blurs the line between right and wrong. Some prosecutors are corrupted by their aspirations to earn more money or ascend the ladder to prestigious jobs, such as district attorney, judge, or a partner in a private law firm. The road to get there is sometimes paved with the blood of criminal convictions of innocent men and women. Justice is often the surest victim in these circumstances.

In this chapter we will look at nine additional true crime stories through the lens of overzealous prosecution. In each case, the criminals were actually guilty; however, the prosecutor sought punishments that were cruel, excessive, and unreasonable by any standard definition. The purpose of this chapter is not to demonize the prosecutors, but to reveal the brutal, unforgiving nature of America's criminal justice system. The idea that as citizens we are entitled to constitutional rights that protect our liberty is an illusion. Nearly all of our laws and rules are open to interpretation, and thus to arbitrary enforcement.

Petty Crimes & Youth Offenses Are Strikes
One of the most insidious laws in California is the Three Strikes Law. Under this abomination, a person must be sentenced to 25 years to life if they have been convicted of three separate crimes. This law was passed in 1994 under the guise that all three crimes had to be either serious or violent. Unfortunately, most voters didn't take the time to read the fine print. The courts have held that the law in fact applies to non-violent, non-serious offenses, as well as juvenile offenses. One of the CROP members named Kevin was actually "struck out" for committing three non-violent, non-serious crimes.

Kevin committed his first crime when he was 16 years old. He and a couple of buddies ordered a pizza delivery to an abandoned apartment. When the pizza deliveryman arrived, the boys took the pizza and locked the door, leaving the deliveryman standing outside. Then, they ran out of the back of the apartment. Kevin was arrested and charged with "Strong Arm Robbery." He signed a plea agreement to plead guilty to that serious crime, because there was no jail time assessed, even though technically he was guilty of a non-violent, non-serious crime. Strike one.

At age 17, Kevin was arrested for stealing something from a parked car. Again, he pleaded guilty to an overinflated charge in a plea agreement that offered him no jail time. Strike two.

At age 22, Kevin was arrested for the crime of Accessory to Attempted Robbery. Kevin and his friend Tommy purchased tobacco from a smoke shop, and were walking down the sidewalk. Tommy said, "That smoke shop is an easy mark. I'm going to rob it. Do you want in?"

"No," Kevin answered. "I'll pass."

Tommy attempted to rob a smoke shop with a gun that wasn't loaded. The shopkeeper responded by reaching for his own gun. Tommy bolted out of the shop and ran away. Kevin was later arrested by a police officer who recognized him from the smoke shop's surveillance video. The prosecutors on the case offered to drop the attempted armed robbery charges if Kevin would tell them where they could find Tommy and testify against him. Kevin refused because he knew he wasn't guilty. Tommy was his friend, and he refused to rat him out. Kevin was tried and convicted of accessory to attempted armed robbery. Strike three. He was sentenced to 25-years to life in state prison. (It should be noted that Kevin's first two strikes were based on plea agreements that occurred when he was a juvenile, and prior to the enactment of the Three Strikes Law.)

Danny The Drug Dealer

Danny Moreno was an obese teenager. When he entered high school at age 13, he weighed over 300 pounds. Danny was teased a lot because of his weight. He felt like an outcast and had difficulty making friends.

Danny was exposed to a number of humiliating social experiences because of his obesity. When he was 11 years old, his mother signed him up for a football league. At the weigh-in he was told that he was too big to play with kids his own age.

His experience at his first school dance was even worse. Danny went shopping with his mother to buy the perfect outfit, and even got a haircut. Danny arrived at the dance with high expectations, but none of the girls would dance with him. They called him fat, and mocked him for even asking.

A breaking point came after Danny went with his mother to the state fair. The next day at school he was harassed by other kids because he attended the fair with his mother, and didn't have any friends. Danny started getting into fist fights with kids who made fun of him because of his obesity. He was in so many fights that he was eventually expelled from public school, and had to attend a continuation school for kids with special needs.

At the continuation school, the popular kids were the ones in the local gang. Danny saw that nobody ever messed with them and that they all had girlfriends. Danny longed for that respect and acceptance. He soon joined the gang. It wasn't difficult; gangs will accept anybody. All you have to do is get "beat down" and you are in.

The other gang members valued Danny because he was a skillful fighter. Danny was consumed with anger and rage because of all the abuse he had endured as a result of his weight problems. Danny beat up other kids because he was hurting inside, and because he was searching for an identity. His peers praised him for his acts of violence. They gave Danny the nickname "Stomper" because he could stomp anybody in a fight. Danny had never been praised by his classmates before, and it felt good. It also felt good to fight and let out his anger. It felt even better to finally be accepted by a group of kids his age.

Danny gradually got involved in the drug game, and he became an enforcer for his gang. If someone didn't pay their drug debts, Stomper would pay them a visit. Danny loved dealing drugs, because having drugs meant that everybody wanted to hang out with him. He even started having girlfriends.

Danny developed a false sense of self-esteem based on his status as a gang member and drug dealer. Between the ages of 18 and 25, Danny was arrested on five separate occasions. Two of the arrests were for assault and battery related to fighting with rival gang members. The other three arrests were drug related. He was continuously incarcerated; never free for more than 90 days at a time. Every time he was released from prison, he returned to the gangs and drug dealing, because that was the source of his self-esteem.

The cycle ended shortly after the Three Strikes Law was enacted. Danny was arrested for holding a tenth of a gram of speed. The prosecutor went for the jugular. No plea bargain was offered. Danny was tried, convicted, and given the mandatory sentence of 25 years to life in prison. The jury was not even aware of the fact that it was a Three Strikes case.

Danny's case is not unique. More than 4,000 men and women are currently serving life sentences in California for petty crimes or drug offenses under the Three Strikes Law. When I was incarcerated, I met men who had been "struck out" and given life sentences for things such as stealing a package of Huggies Diapers from the supermarket, check fraud, and possession of a stolen license plate, among other ridiculous non-violent crimes.

A Crime of Passion

Tyler James was a deeply religious man. Throughout his youth, Tyler was an altar boy who went to weekly Bible study classes. He attended a Catholic grade school, a Catholic high school, and a Catholic university. He graduated from Notre Dame with a degree in computer science and went on to build a successful software business.

At Notre Dame, Tyler fell in love with Britney Myers. They married and were blessed with four happy children. Tyler became a deacon in the local church and was a member of the Rotary Club. He joined the National Guard. He always donated 10 percent of his annual earnings to the church and an additional 10 percent to local charities. He was considered a pillar in the community by everyone who knew him. Yet, all was not right in Tyler's seemingly perfect world. Unbeknownst to Tyler, Britney was having an affair with his business partner.

One afternoon Tyler came home unexpectedly and caught Britney and his business partner having sex. Tyler went ballistic, and immediately went into the garage to get his hunting rifle. In the meantime, Tyler's business partner got dressed and made a break for it. Tyler shot his partner in the leg as he was running down the driveway. The man fell to the ground and screamed in agony. Without saying a word, Tyler walked over to his partner, raised the rifle, and shot him right between the eyes. The man died instantly. Tyler then got into his truck, drove directly to the police station, and turned himself in.

Based on the standard set forth in the California Penal Code, Tyler's case was a textbook example of voluntary manslaughter. It was not premeditated. Yet, the Los Angeles County District Attorney's Office charged Tyler with first-degree murder. During the ensuing trial the D.A. used flimsy, circumstantial evidence to argue that Tyler already knew about the affair and that the murder was premeditated. Tyler's defense was this crime was voluntary manslaughter. The jury compromised, as they often do, finding Tyler guilty of second-degree murder.

At the sentencing hearing, the prosecutor argued that Tyler should be sentenced to 40 years to life — the mandatory sentence of 15 years to life for second-degree murder and additional 25 years to life for the gun enhancement, based on a new law enacted for gang members, drive-by shootings, and such. Tyler's judge felt the enhancement was excessive due to the circumstances of the case. She then proceeded to apply a more reasonable sentence enhancement that added four years to the sentence. Tyler was sentenced to 19 years to life in state prison.

The D.A.'s office appealed the judge's decision on the sentencing enhancement to the state appellate court and prevailed. Tyler was remanded back to Superior Court to be resentenced. The trial judge was irate at the prosecutors for undermining her authority. She pounded on her desk as she said, "This sentence is cruel and unusual punishment, unconstitutional, and grossly disproportionate to the defendant's individual culpability and circumstances. But I have been mandated by a higher court, so I am simply a ministerial officer at this point saying the words '40 to life.'"

Tyler hung his head and mumbled, "Why do they even have trial court judges?" He had been burned by an unjust system.

A Father's Revenge

Bethany Giles was a 14-year-old girl with low self-esteem. Kids made fun of Bethany because she had an extremely large nose and terrible acne. Boys called her ugly. She never had a boyfriend and had never even been kissed.

Shortly after she entered high school, Bethany was befriended by a 17-year-old gang member named LaShawn. LaShawn introduced Bethany to drinking and drugs. One night Bethany got so high that she passed out. LaShawn took her clothes off and tied her to the bed. When Bethany regained consciousness, LaShawn was raping her. Bethany screamed and begged LaShawn to stop. When the nightmare was over, LaShawn told Bethany that the sex was consensual; that she did not remember asking him to tie her up because she was so high. Bethany knew he was lying, but quietly concurred with LaShawn so he would allow her to leave.

Bethany was ashamed of what had occurred. She told no one. Over the next month, Bethany slipped into a state of severe depression. She pretended to be ill so she could stay home from school. Bethany didn't want to leave her house.

Bethany's parents knew something wasn't right. They pressed Bethany to tell them what was wrong. Bethany started crying, and between sobs she told them about the rape.

Bethany's father, Charlie, was incensed. He took matters into his own hands. Instead of going to the police, Charlie loaded his gun, went to LaShawn's house and killed him.

Like Tyler James, Charlie Giles was a model citizen. He was a 66-year-old retired fireman and father of six. Despite the circumstances, and Charlie's distinguished 25-year career as a civil servant, the San Diego County prosecutor's office charged him with first-degree murder. During the trial, the prosecutor presented its case for premeditation and malice of forethought. However, Bethany's emotional testimony about the rape and her father's devotion won the day. The jury found Charlie guilty of the lesser charge of voluntary manslaughter.

At the sentencing hearing, the prosecutor argued the case merited a 25-year to life sentence enhancement for the use of the gun, despite the fact that the new gun enhancement law did not apply to manslaughter. The California Penal Code states the sentence for voluntary manslaughter shall be three, six or 11 years and that first-time offenders shall be sentenced to the mid-term. The range for the gun enhancement associated with manslaughter is an additional three, four, or 10 years, and the sentence is at the discretion of the trial judge. Charlie was given the maximum sentence 16 years, of which he must serve 85 percent. Charlie will not be eligible for parole until he is 80 years of age. Charlie's was truly a good news/bad news story. He received the benefit of the lesser charge of manslaughter, yet was slapped with the maximum sentence possible. Fair? You be the judge.

The Burglar's Surprise

Luke Sanders was a happy, well-adjusted 13-year-old boy. He played sports, received good grades in school, and obeyed his parents. On the weekends Luke did fun things, such as archery, fishing, or dirt bike riding with his father, whom he loved immensely.

An unforeseen tragedy occurred in Luke's family. Luke's father killed himself. He did not even leave a note. No one knew why he committed suicide, and Luke blamed himself. He felt rejected, unloved, and alone in the world.

Luke's mother suffered financially after the loss of her husband. They were required to move from a nice house into a low-income neighborhood. Luke had to wear his brother's hand-me-down clothes because there wasn't enough money to buy new clothes. There was scarcely any food in the refrigerator. They were poor, and Luke didn't like it at all.

Luke eventually started shoplifting food and clothes. In the beginning, he only stole the things he needed. Then, he became addicted to the adrenaline rush involved in the crime. In Luke's mind, it was thrilling to steal things. When one gets away with it, one becomes more brazen. If one starts the pattern of breaking the law and doesn't get caught, the problem will grow and become out of control. That's what happened with Luke.

When Luke was 16 years old, he started hanging out with a hoodlum named Tony who burglarized houses. Tony told Luke that it was easy money and asked if Luke would like to become his crime partner. Tony bragged about several scores he had made by breaking into houses in nice neighborhoods. Tony's "foolproof" scheme involved going to the front door and knocking. If no one was home and there was no alarm system, Tony would go around to the back of the house and break a window to enter. Luke eagerly agreed to become Tony's partner.

Luke and Tony soon burglarized a home in the upscale Woodland Hills neighborhood north of Los Angeles. They were in the house for about 10 minutes. Tony was upstairs looking through one bedroom, while Luke ransacked another bedroom on the ground floor. The couple who owned the house returned while the boys were inside.

Luke heard the front door unlock. There was no way to alert Tony without giving away his own position. Luke slipped out of the bedroom window and ran like his feet were on fire.

A few minutes later as he waited for Tony, he heard a gunshot. Then he heard three more shots. Luke later learned that Tony had discovered the couple's handgun while burglarizing their bedroom. When the home owners cornered him in the upstairs bedroom, Tony panicked and shot them both.

Tony and Luke were both arrested based on fingerprints that were found at the scene of the crime. The police found the murder weapon in Tony's apartment. Despite the fact that Luke was only 16 years old, he was tried as an adult. The charge was two counts of first-degree murder in the commission of a burglary. The prosecutor was seeking the death penalty. The facts that Luke did not intend to hurt anyone and didn't carry a weapon were deemed irrelevant. The prosecutor knew the couple had been shot with their own gun and that Tony was the shooter. The facts of the case were fairly obvious. Nevertheless, Luke was prosecuted to the full extent of the law as if he had been the shooter. Luke and Tony were both found equally guilty of two counts of first-degree murder and sentenced to life in prison without the possibility of parole.

High School Parties Are Dangerous
Timo Moeatu was born and raised on the Hawaiian island of Oahu. Timo's passion was playing football. His dream was to play in the National Football League when he grew up. To increase his exposure to college scouts and his chances of earning a football scholarship, Timo moved to Anaheim, California, where he lived with relatives during his senior year in high school.

Timo's cousins, Junior and Troy, were members of a Samoan gang called the Ace Treys. Timo readily joined the gang and became involved in dealing drugs. Timo had friends in Hawaii who grew high-grade marijuana. He began to import large quantities of pot from Hawaii, which the other gang members sold.

Timo liked the easy money he made importing and selling drugs, and he loved hanging out with his homies, but he did not allow those activities to deter him from his long-range goal of playing professional football. Timo became the star linebacker for his high school football team and earned a full scholarship to Ohio State University.

At Ohio State, Timo won the job as the starting middle linebacker during his freshman year. He led the team in tackles and appeared to be on the fast track to achieving his dream of becoming a professional athlete. The team's 11-1 record earned them a trip to the Rose Bowl, a New Year's Day game played in Los Angeles.

The team traveled to Los Angeles the day after Christmas, giving them four days to prepare for the game. Timo asked his coach for permission to spend one night with his family in nearby Anaheim. When he was denied, Timo decided to sneak out of the dorm one evening to attend a party with his cousins.

Timo, Junior, Troy, another Ace Trey gang member named Flacco, and four of their home girls piled into two cars and went to the party. There was plenty of booze, pot, and pretty girls. Timo was having a fun time until several members of the rival 13th Street gang arrived at the party.

The 13th Street gang is a Mexican gang. Several boys from the gang picked on Flacco, a Mexican kid, who chose to join a Samoan gang instead of the 13th Street gang. A fight broke out between Flacco and one of the 13th Street gang members. A melee ensued, and Timo was right in the middle of it. The fighting lasted for several minutes before the Ace Trey gang members and their home girls made the decision to get out of there. They jumped into their cars and sped away.

In the confusion and rush to leave the party, the Ace Trey gang members left a home girl named Lola behind. Lola was in the back bedroom making out with someone when the fighting commenced. The Ace Trey boys feared for Lola's safety and returned to the party to retrieve her.

Troy pulled up in front of the house. The party was still raging. He honked the horn. Junior, Flacco, and Timo got out of the car and made their way across the front lawn. The door swung open.

"It's them!" one of the 13th Street gang members yelled.

"We just came back to get Lola," Timo said. "We don't

want any problems."

"Fuck you, punk," one of the 13th Street gang members replied. "Let's get them," he exclaimed, leading a charge of seven gang members.

A second melee ensued. Timo was taken to the ground and kicked in the face by several gang members. Junior leaped to his defense, yielding a four-inch buck knife. He stabbed one of the kids four times and another eight times. Both boys died on the spot.

Junior, Troy, Flacco, and Timo were all charged with two counts of first-degree (premeditated) murder. They all faced life in prison without the possibility of parole. At trial, the boys' attorneys presented the truth of what occurred that night as their principal defense. Junior, Troy and Flacco were all convicted of the "lesser" charge of voluntary manslaughter and sentenced to 11 years each in prison. Timo's attorney distinguished his client by calling his high school and college football coaches to testify about his stellar character. The strategy paid off. Eleven of the jurors voted to acquit Timo, but one juror held out for manslaughter. It resulted in a hung jury.

As was his option, the Orange County prosecutor elected to retry Timo on the two counts of first-degree murder. In Timo's second trial, the prosecutor presented a new theory: the murders were the result of a drug deal gone bad. They presented witnesses from Timo's high school and from Ohio State University who testified that Timo was a drug dealer. Even though there was absolutely no evidence that drugs were a factor in the fights or the murders, the prosecutor was successful in hoodwinking the jury. Timo was convicted of two counts of second-degree murder and sentenced to 30-years to life in state prison. In one dangerous night of partying, all of Timo's dreams were smashed.

Parties Are Dangerous – Case II
Chad Bennett, a 22-year-old radiologist, had just landed his dream job working at Children's Hospital in Los Angeles. Working three, 12-hour shifts per week left him ample free time for surfing, hiking, and climbing. Chad loved the outdoors. On Sundays, he enjoyed cooking on an outdoor grill in his backyard and partying

with friends.

One Sunday afternoon, Chad invited about 20 family members and friends to his place for a barbecue and beer. Everyone was drinking and having a good time. Chad was in the backyard chatting with guests and tending to the grill. He was unaware that an uninvited man named Raul had arrived at the party.

Raul was the estranged ex-boyfriend of Chad's younger sister, Penny. Penny and Raul had a four-month-old son named Kelly. They had lived together for two years and had planned to get married. Then, following Kelly's birth, Raul started drinking heavily and doing drugs. The responsibility of being a father and provider overwhelmed him. At that point, Penny left Raul, and she and Kelly moved in with Chad.

Raul was intoxicated when he arrived at Chad's home that afternoon. He accused Penny of cheating on him with a friend named Taylor, who was also at the party. When Taylor took offense to the infidelity allegations, a fist fight erupted.

The two young men were going at it in the living room when Chad entered the house. The music was blaring, Penny was screaming at Raul, and Chad's furniture was being broken. Chad was under the influence of alcohol and was not thinking rationally. He opened a drawer and removed a small 22-caliber pistol, which he kept in case of intruders.

"Stop fighting in my house!" Chad screamed, pointing the pistol at the two men.

Taylor pulled away from Raul, who was still shouting obscenities.

Penny stepped between the two men and shoved Raul toward the door. "Get out!" she yelled.

At that exact moment the gun went off. A single bullet grazed Penny's forearm and hit Raul mid-chest. He collapsed to the floor. In the process of pulling away from Raul, Taylor had shoved into another guest named Mark, who in turn slammed into Chad. Chad's finger had been on the trigger when he was bumped and the gun went off accidentally.

Penny immediately called 911. When Raul's heart stopped beating, Chad performed CPR, but to no avail. Chad was covered in Raul's blood when the police arrived on the scene. Chad took the remaining bullets out of the gun and placed it in the middle of the coffee table. He walked out of the house with his hands raised over his head, lay on the front lawn and put his hands behind his back.

A dozen witnesses gave statements to the events described above. Nevertheless, the Los Angeles County District Attorney's Office charged Chad with first-degree murder, with a special gun enhancement allegation. Chad was facing 50-years to life in prison. Chad's defense attorney planned to call to the stand all of the partygoers as witnesses, and argue that Chad was not guilty of any crime, that the shooting was an accident. However, there was a gaping hole in the defense's case. Mark had fled the scene before the police arrived, because he was on parole and did not want to be returned to prison for a parole violation. Mark's testimony that he ran into Chad was crucial to prove that the shooting was accidental; yet, Mark absconded.

Chad's attorney filed various motions to delay the trial. His hope was that Mark would eventually be arrested for violating his parole, but that never happened. Meanwhile, the stress of the potential murder trial was tearing Chad's mother apart. She suffered a heart attack at a pretrial hearing and barely survived.

Two days before the trial was to commence, the prosecutor offered Chad a plea bargain: Chad would plead guilty to manslaughter and accept a nine-year sentence, of which he would be required to serve a minimum of seven years and seven months. Chad did not want to accept the "deal," because he knew he was not guilty. Chad had never committed a crime in his life. A guilty plea would destroy his medical career. Yet, Chad's mother told him the stress of a murder trial might just kill her. She couldn't bear the thought of her son spending the rest of his life behind bars. Chad reluctantly signed the plea agreement for the nine-year sentence.

The Beautiful Drug Addict

Kiki Rodriguez was a beautiful, 13-year-old girl who was raped at that tender age by her uncle. The tragedy was emotionally crippling. From that point on, Kiki remained fearful of men and had difficulty developing relationships with boys her own age.

When Kiki was in high school, she started smoking pot. Kiki discovered that when she got high, her fear of interacting with boys disappeared. Kiki smoked pot before school every day, during the lunch hour, and after school. This behavior continued into college, where Kiki began experimenting with hard drugs.

At age 19, Kiki fell in love with a graduate student named Jake Thomas, who did not use drugs. She introduced Jake to smoking pot, and he liked it. Together they started doing Oxycodone and Jake quickly became addicted. The couple then graduated to heroin. At first they snorted the heroin, and then they experimented with mainlining (using a needle to inject the drug directly into their bloodstream). The amount of heroin required to get the couple high continued to increase as their addictions worsened.

One evening Jake purchased a quarter ounce of China White heroine and invited Kiki over to his dorm room to party. Jake loaded the syringe with a half gram of heroin, which was the amount they typically used at that stage of their addictions. Kiki slipped a tie around Jake's bicep and tightened the noose. The veins running inside Jake's forearm engorged with blood. Kiki put the needle into Jake's arm and pressed down on the syringe plunger. Jake drifted off into a serene state of euphoria.

"Babe, that was the most intense rush I've ever experienced," Jake said as he watched Kiki prepare a shot for herself. "This China White is heavy. To be safe, I think you should start with a quarter."

"Better safe than dead," Kiki teased as she drew a quarter gram of heroin into the syringe.

Jake slipped the tie around Kiki's arm. She opened and closed her hand into a fist several times to drive blood into her veins. When they were engorged, Jake pierced her skin with the needle and administered the shot.

"Oh my God!" Kiki exclaimed.

They were the last words she would ever utter. Kiki collapsed into Jake's arms and died instantly.

Jake called 911, but the paramedics arrived too late to accomplish anything. The police arrived shortly thereafter and Jake was arrested. The Orange County DA's office should have charged

Jake with involuntary manslaughter, which is defined in the California Penal Code as "engaging in an illegal activity that results in the unintentional death of a human being." However, prosecutors in the state of California operate with complete disregard of justice and the rules of law. Jake was charged with first-degree murder. Attempts by Jake's attorney to negotiate a plea bargain were rebuffed. There would be no deals offered.

During the trial, prosecutors attempted to portray Jake as a money-grubbing drug dealer with no conscience. They produced two witnesses who purchased heroin from Jake. They argued that Jake had introduced Kiki to heroin so she would purchase drugs from him on a continuous basis.

Fortunately, Jake's parents were able to hire an exceptional attorney, who put on a first-rate defense. On cross-examination, both star witnesses admitted they had to beg and plead with Jake to get him to sell them the drugs and that he was not a known drug dealer. The trial turned on the testimony of two witnesses: Stacy, Kiki's sister; and Dr. Frank Baller, a forensics expert.

Stacy was the star witness for the prosecution. She was originally called to testify that Jake was the first person to give heroin to Kiki, but Stacy was a reluctant witness. She did not want to testify against Jake, because she knew her sister had been madly in love with him. On cross-examination, Stacy turned hostile toward the prosecution. She testified that Kiki had a long history of drug use and that, in fact, Kiki had introduced Jake to pot and had gotten him involved with Oxycodone.

Dr. Baller's testimony revealed important facts about hidden dangers of which all drug users should be aware. He testified, "Drug dealers are not pharmacists. Most have no idea what they're doing. Dangerous chemicals that can, and do, cause death are used to transform poppy seeds into heroin. Also, the concentrations of opiates are not balanced properly in heroin production. It's entirely possible that the quarter gram of heroin Kiki injected possessed 10 times the concentration of opiates as the half gram of heroin that Jake injected. There was no way Jake could have known how much opium Kiki was receiving."

Following Dr. Baller's testimony, the prosecutor offered Jake a plea bargain for second-degree murder with a sentence of 15 years to life in prison. Jake's attorney scoffed at the ridiculous plea offer and derided the prosecutor for overzealous prosecution. The next day the prosecutor offered voluntary manslaughter, 11 years. Jake's attorney made a counter-offer; involuntary manslaughter, three years probation, no prison time. The prosecutor's ego would not allow him to agree to such a fair plea-bargain. The case would have to be decided by the jury, but not before Jake's emotional testimony.

Through tear-filled eyes, Jake told the jury that Kiki was the love of his life and that he had hoped to marry her and spend the rest of his life with her. Jake admitted he had purchased the heroin that killed her, and that he had put the needle in her arm. He further admitted that he was responsible for Kiki's death and he hoped her family and God would find it in their hearts to forgive him someday.

The jury only deliberated for 45 minutes before rendering a verdict of guilty for involuntary manslaughter. During the sentencing phase, the prosecutor argued that Jake should be given the maximum sentence of six years in prison. Jake's attorney argued for probation. The judge sentenced Jake to four years, the mid-term sentence prescribed in the sentencing guidelines.

Dr. Lance the Alcoholic
Lance Ryan was intelligent, caring, and compassionate. He was class valedictorian both in high school and in college. He finished first in his class in medical school. Lance became a wealthy, successful doctor who was adored by his patients. Yet, Lance was still not happy.

About the time Lance entered high school; he realized that he was different from most of his classmates. Lance was gay. He was picked on, bullied, called names, and beat up almost every day in high school. No one seemed to care about his pain and suffering. No one could protect him; especially not his father, who was a strict military man. His father shamed Lance by ignoring him or telling him that something was wrong with him. Lance's mother treated him the same way. He received no love from his family and he had no friends.

Lance drowned his sorrows in alcohol. He started drinking

in high school, and by the time he entered college he was getting drunk every evening. As an adult, Lance became a functioning alcoholic. During the day when he was at school, and later at work, he was sober. Every evening he got blind drunk. When people are under the influence of alcohol, they generally make poor decisions.

One night after work, Lance drove to a bar and got snockered. While driving home, he was involved in a horrible automobile accident. A mother, father, teenage boy, and a teenage girl were in the other car. Everyone died except for the teenage girl, who was left paralyzed from the waist down. Lance had two prior drunk driving convictions on his record. He was tried and convicted of three counts of second-degree murder and sentenced to 15 years to life in state prison.

Lance's story provides an important lesson for anyone who has ever been convicted of driving under the influence of alcohol. If you drive drunk again and kill someone, you will be tried and most likely be convicted of second-degree murder, which carries a mandatory sentence of 15 years to life in prison.

In the old Canon Book of Legal Ethics all law students are taught, "A prosecutor's job is not to convict, but to see that justice is served." Yet, district attorneys and prosecutors stopped following this moral directive in the late 1980s as a result of the "Willie Horton affair."

Willie Horton was a life term inmate in the state of Massachusetts who was released during Michael Dukakis' stint as the state's governor. Just one week following his release, Horton raped and murdered a woman, and also killed her husband. When Dukakis ran for president years later, his opponent, George Bush, Sr., promoted a tough-on-crime campaign that centered on the Willie Horton affair. Bush used negative TV commercials which depicted Dukakis as soft on crime because, as governor, he had signed Horton's furlough papers. Pre-election polls revealed a massive 25-point swing in voter opinion in favor of Bush as a direct result of the TV commercials. The event ushered in a new era of tough-on-crime politics. Politicians at all levels — governors, district attorneys, mayors, state legislation, etc. — used tough-on-crime platforms to win elections. Politicians routinely sponsored harsh new sentencing laws, such as the Three Strikes Law and the 25-year gun enhancement laws described in this chapter to advance their political careers. Such unjust laws serve no purpose in deterring crime. Their true purpose was to provide media opportunities for selfless politicians seeking election or reelection.

The era of tough-on-crime politics also corrupted America's criminal justice system. The only way any attorney general or district attorney could be reelected was by pursuing overzealous prosecution in every case. If they let their guard down on a single case, they knew that political opponents would seize the moment to portray them as soft on crime. The end result is the senseless incarceration of many thousands of men and women all across the country. Between 1989 (the year the Willie Horton ads first appeared on TV) until 2010, the number of people incarcerated in American prisons grew from 773,919 to 2,266,800. Additionally, 4,933,667 people were on probation or parole. A total of 7,225,800 were under supervision (prison, jail, parole or probation). These numbers are staggering and tragic.

This book concludes with some rather obvious lessons. Don't break the law — *any* law. Don't cheat on your taxes. Don't do drugs. Don't even consider jaywalking or speeding. Take pride in being a law abiding citizen. That is something to be proud of.

One never knows what the consequences of one's acts will be. When one commits a crime — no matter how innocent the act may seem — one has no concept whatsoever of the long-range or indirect consequences. Who are the victims? How will the crime impact their lives? What about the victims' families and friends? Are there any innocent bystanders who might end up in harm's way? When one commits a single crime, one generally does not consider any of these questions, and the failure to do so generally has disastrous results.

Acknowledgements

This book would not have been possible without the contributions of the CROP members and other prisoners who allowed me to tell their stories. Many thanks to Rodwick, Matt, Tim, Jake, Jim, Johnny, Joe, Diego, Kevin, Danny, Tyler, Charlie, Luke, Chad, Lance, and the many other convicts who allowed me to interview them but preferred to remain nameless.

I would also like to thank Sly and Maury for their insights into gangs. Although these men elected to not have their stories appear in the book, they provided most of the information about why kids join gangs, what to expect when you join a gang and how to get out of a gang. These were immense contributions that I believe will help countless teens make better choices.

Special thanks go to my editors, typist and proofreaders. Editors James Bottomley and Cris Wanzer are both talented wordsmiths who elevated this book to a level of professionalism far beyond my capabilities. My mom, Jackie, typed the manuscript and provided invaluable instructive criticism along the way. Chris Martinez, Pat Covey, Ted Swain, Mike Hansen, Jason Anderson, Ron Woodhill, Pat Stewart, Jeff Moon, and Becky Moon all proofread the book, and offered important insights. Extra special thanks goes to Nikki Marcano whose eye for detail is unparalleled. Nikki caught numerous typos and errors that I had missed and that would have negatively affected the book's credibility.

Finally, I have to thank Armando Villalobos for the awesome book cover design.

About The Author

My book *The Dirty Nasty Truth: 18 True Crime Stories & 10 Life in Prison Stories to Stop Juvenile Delinquency* provides penetrating insight into the criminal mind. Teachers, juvenile justice personnel and organizations concerned with at-risk youth endorse the book as a powerful tool for deterring delinquency. My status as an ex-con, delinquency intervention speaker/counselor, and researcher who interviewed more than 100 criminals, gives me a singular perspective on the root causes of criminal behavior.

I am a recovering outlaw who spent the last 20 years studying books on personal growth and human achievement. Along the way I took copious notes and compiled all of the most insightful information into a personal excellence program, which serves as my new code of conduct. My quest to overcome my character flaws inspired me to write two self-improvement books – *Penitentiary Fitness: The Amazing Weight Loss Formula* and *Dare to Be Successful: A Parable to Find Meaning in Life.*

My passion is entrepreneurship and my mission is to focus that passion on marketing my books, as well as other products and services that aspire to enrich people's lives.

I currently reside in Southern California where I work as a public speaker and delinquency prevention specialist.

I am also a book shepherd and the author of the popular e-book *Self-Publishing on Amazon.com*. If you or someone you know is interested in having their book published, I can help. Visit my website www.johnbarretthawkins.com, or e-mail me at:

johnbarretthawkins@gmail.com.

DARE TO BE SUCCESSFUL

Dare to Be Successful is a parable about a middle school teacher who helps female gang member transform her life. The story will teach you how to discover your purpose, increase your self-confidence, overcome daily challenges, and fulfill your dreams.

Dare to Be Successful is based on John Barrett Hawkins' 15-year study of human achievement. Included are teachings from Wayne Dyer, Napoleon Hill, Cheryl Richardson, Marianne Williamson, Stephen Covey, Martha Beck, Mark Viktor Hansen, Jack Canfield, Og Mandino, Anthony Robbins, Deepak Chopra and Caroline Myss, among others. This book spells out 75 principles used by the world's most successful people. You'll discover:

- Tools that will enable you to identify your natural talents and ideal career
- Secrets for developing a winning mindset and becoming unstoppable
- Strategies for mastering your emotions
- A detailed action plan for setting and achieving your goals
- Tips to overcome procrastination and stay motivated
- Techniques to recondition your belief system and eliminate the behaviors may be preventing you from fulfilling your dreams

Dare to Be Successful reveals the philosophies and habits of the world's peak performers…and provides a step-by-step process to help you create the successful life you deserve.

– Also by John Barrett Hawkins –

PENITENTIARY FITNESS

When the California Department of Corrections took away their weights, the inmates created an ingenious exercise regimen using their own body weight. The push-up and pull-up type workouts enabled them to develop sleek, muscular physiques remarkably similar to those of Olympic gymnasts. Author John Barrett Hawkins immediately recognized that people in the "real world" would benefit from these training methods and set out to write *PENITENTIARY FITNESS.*

With no professional credentials to speak of, Hawkins decided to base the book's recommendations on the findings of leading fitness and weight-loss authors and on research studies that were conducted at the world's top medical schools and universities. Over a 10-year period he studied hundreds of resources on the subjects of weight loss and fitness and applied that knowledge to the convict's unique style of training. The result is *THE AMAZING WEIGHT LOSS FORMULA.*

You will find:
- Medical Sciences 20 Fat Loss Secrets
- Cutting-edge strategies for men who want to build rock-hard muscles
- Proven tactics for women who want to trim their tummy or derrière
- An in-depth discussion on nutrition, plus a diet plan that will empower you to lose weight while eating six meals every day
- 36 delicious, healthy meal recipes
- 16 creative workouts that do not require equipment and can be performed at the park or in the convenience of your own home

PENITENTIARY FITNESS is the one book you need to achieve the body you've always dreamed of having.

179

SELF-PUBLISHING ON AMAZON.COM

John Barrett Hawkins is the author of three self published books *The Dirty Nasty Truth: 18 True Crime Stories to Stop Juvenile Delinquency, Penitentiary Fitness: The Amazing Weight Loss Formula* and *Dare to Be Successful: A Parable to Find Meaning in Life.* In December 2012, the Kindle e-book edition of *The Dirty Nasty Truth* reached #1 in Amazon's Law & Crime category, just four months after publication. In *Self-Publishing on Amazon*, Hawkins tells you how he achieved those results. He also answers these important questions:

* How to publish your e-book with Kindle free of charge
* How to publish your soft cover book with Create Space (aka Amazon.com) free of charge
* How to make your title come up #1 in Amazon search results for specific keywords
* How to create an author website that drives sales
* How to create webinars that inspire people to buy your book
* How to land radio interviews and sell thousands of books
* How to land TV interviews all across the country
* How to create an Amazon #1 bestseller

Self-Publishing on Amazon is the one book you need to achieve success as an author.

Chapter 10: The Gentleman Bank Robber

[1]Covey, Stephen. *The Seven Habits of Highly Effective People.* Simon & Shuster. 1989.

[2]Waitley, Denis. *The Psychology of Winning.* Nightingale Conant 1979.

[3]Alter, John. *The Transformative Power of Crisis.* Regan Books. 2000.

[4]Dyer, Wayne. *The Power of Intention. PBS TV Special.*

[5]Waitley, Denis. *The Psychology of Winning.* Nightingale Conant 1979.

Chapter 11: Overzealous Prosecution

[1] Heath, B. and Kevin McCoy. "Prosecutors Can Tip The Scale" *USA Today.* 9-23-2010. P.1.

Chapter 10: The Gentleman Bank Robber

[1]Covey, Stephen. *The Seven Habits of Highly Effective People.* Simon & Shuster. 1989.

[2]Waitley, Denis. *The Psychology of Winning.* Nightingale Conant 1979.

[3]Alter, John. *The Transformative Power of Crisis.* Regan Books. 2000.

[4]Dyer, Wayne. *The Power of Intention. PBS TV Special.*

[5]Waitley, Denis. *The Psychology of Winning.* Nightingale Conant 1979.

Chapter 11: Overzealous Prosecution

[1] Heath, B. and Kevin McCoy. "Prosecutors Can Tip The Scale" *USA Today.* 9-23-2010. P.1.

Made in the USA
San Bernardino, CA
02 July 2019